"I am very happy to endorse this book with
I have been waiting for Sam to produce this
All aspects of living in fallen-and-yet-to-be-renewed bodies
and biblically addressed with lucid writing that is a pleasure to read. Sam's compassion for all the ways in which people suffer in those fallen bodies is full of
understanding and tenderness. Please read this book with every expectation of
being enlightened and edified."

> **Kathy Keller,** Assistant Director of Communications, Redeemer
> Presbyterian Church, New York City, New York

"One of the most confused aspects of our culture relates to how we see the body.
That confusion often extends to the church, despite the fact that our faith is
centered around the Word who became flesh. In this wise and practical book,
Sam Allberry casts a vision of the body that is neither beastly nor mechanistic
but instead is creaturely and Christ informed. After reading this book, you will
be better equipped to think through questions from eating disorders to the
transgender debate to transhumanism, as well as the more perennial questions
of how to think about 'soul' and 'body' in terms of the gospel. You will come
away with even more awe and wonder at the words of one who said to us, 'This
is my body, broken for you.'"

> **Russell Moore,** President, The Ethics & Religious Liberty Commission of
> the Southern Baptist Convention

"Evangelicals have excelled at many things; theological reflection on the body isn't
one of them. If you're thinking, 'I've seen many books on the church!' then your
assumption proves my point. Far more attention has been devoted to Christ's
spiritual body than to our physical selves. But we desperately need guidance here,
for we inhabit a confused age that waffles back and forth between body obsession
(my body is the most important thing about me) and body denial (my body is
irrelevant to who I really am). Feel the whiplash? This book is medicine for the
moment. I'm thrilled it now exists."

> **Matt Smethurst,** Managing Editor, The Gospel Coalition; author,
> *Deacons* and *Before You Open Your Bible*

"This book is good news for everybody, everywhere. There is a plethora of books written by women about the body these days, but men have bodies too, and a perspective on them that is often overlooked. I commend Sam's words to everyone who needs to think more about their body and the bodies of others."

Lore Ferguson Wilbert, author, *Handle with Care: How Jesus Redeems the Power of Touch in Life and Ministry*

"Winsome. Quotable. Simultaneously relevant and timeless. *What God Has to Say about Our Bodies* manages to be both deeply positive and hopeful about our bodies while also being deeply compassionate toward those who suffer in their bodies, especially with broken bodily longings. Clearly forged through long years of honest conversations in the pastorate, Allberry embraces the hard questions, gives wise and measured guidance, and will convince and inspire you with his core thesis: 'We can trust Christ with our bodies.'"

Alasdair Groves, Executive Director, Christian Counseling & Educational Foundation; coauthor, *Untangling Emotions*

"Pastor-theologian Sam Allberry has given a gift to the church: a volume full of texture and beauty related to God making us enfleshed persons. For far too long, evangelicals have neglected the significance of the body as an integral part of our embodiment and discipleship. So much of the current cultural confusion persists, both inside and outside the church, because we've misunderstood the gift of the body and the message it would teach us about God. Sam Allberry has ably remedied that gap. Read this book."

Andrew T. Walker, Associate Professor of Christian Ethics, The Southern Baptist Theological Seminary; Fellow, The Ethics and Public Policy Center

What God Has to Say about Our Bodies

What God Has to Say about Our Bodies

How the Gospel Is Good News for Our Physical Selves

Sam Allberry

Foreword by Paul David Tripp

∷ CROSSWAY®

WHEATON, ILLINOIS

Trade paperback ISBN: 978-1-4335-7015-5
ePub ISBN: 978-1-4335-7018-6
PDF ISBN: 978-1-4335-7016-2
Mobipocket ISBN: 978-1-4335-7017-9

Library of Congress Cataloging-in-Publication Data

Names: Allberry, Sam, author.
Title: What God has to say about our bodies : how the gospel is good news for our physical selves / Sam Allberry ; foreword by Paul David Tripp.
Description: Wheaton, Illinois : Crossway, [2021] | Includes bibliographical references and indexes.
Identifiers: LCCN 2020044051 (print) | LCCN 2020044052 (ebook) | ISBN 9781433570155 (trade paperback) | ISBN 9781433570162 (pdf) | ISBN 9781433570179 (mobi) | ISBN 9781433570186 (epub)
Subjects: LCSH: Human body—Religious aspects—Christianity. | Human body—Biblical teaching.
Classification: LCC BT741.3 .A45 2021 (print) | LCC BT741.3 (ebook) | DDC 233/.5—dc23
LC record available at https://lccn.loc.gov/2020044051
LC ebook record available at https://lccn.loc.gov/2020044052

Crossway is a publishing ministry of Good News Publishers.

BP		30	29	28	27	26	25	24	23	22	21
15	14	13	12	11	10	9	8	7	6	5	4	3	2	1

To my favorite body of all, the church
family at Immanuel Nashville.
Thank you for continuing to make Jesus
non-ignorable to me, week by week,
through gospel teaching and gospel culture.
I love you.

Contents

Foreword

THERE IS AN INHERENT DANGER in writing a foreword for a book you haven't written: you consent to write the foreword before reading the book. But I agreed without any fear because I know Sam Allberry, and I have enormous respect for the depth, clarity, and practicality of his gospel voice.

I have good news for you—the book you're about to read is not only good, culturally relevant, and easy to read, but it is also an essential book. This book should be on the desk of every pastor, ministry leader, parent, or any Christian who wants to think their way through the body confusion of this moment in the human community.

I want to tell you why this is such an important book. The gospel of Jesus Christ is profoundly more than a message about our entrance and our exit. Often the gospel gets reduced to the "gospel past," that moment when, by grace, we saw our sin and trusted in Christ for our forgiveness and reconciliation to God. Or the gospel is lessened to only the "gospel future," the glorious destiny that is secured for us by grace. Many believers have a pretty good grasp of the gospel past and the gospel future, but they live with a significant gap in the middle of their gospel. They don't understand how the present implications of the person and work of the gospel change how to think about and respond to everything right here, right now. Sadly, many Christians suffer from living in a relatively constant state of gospel amnesia, the fruit of which can be seen all around us.

Much of my writing has sought to unpack the *now-ism* of the gospel of Jesus Christ for married couples, parents, Christian leaders, and those going through midlife or suffering and in the areas of sexuality and money. The gospel is that profound narrative of God's redeeming grace in Christ Jesus, and that narrative provides a way for us to see everything in life. Between the "already" of our conversion and the "not yet" of our homegoing, the gospel of Jesus Christ is the world's best hermeneutic—that is, the best interpretive tool God has ever given. It is how we make sense of ourselves and all that we encounter as we journey through the broken world that is our present address. It may sound trite, but I tell people all the time to put on their gospel glasses and take another look at something in their life and see how it looks different to them when they look through the lens of the gospel.

I don't think there is a better example of what I have just described than *What God Has to Say about Our Bodies*. The brilliance of this book is that it enables you to look through the lens of the gospel at an issue that has never been more culturally and spiritually important—the body. In so doing, it cuts through the cultural confusion and gives us clarity as to who we are as creatures made in God's image. And what I appreciate so much is that as Sam does this, there is not a hint of theological arrogance, no pseudo-Christian snarkiness, no trivializing of the deep identity struggles of others, or no war with the culture. This book is shaped not just by the *message* of the gospel but also by the *character* of the gospel, which makes it even more approachable, convicting, encouraging, motivating, and hope giving.

I have spent much of my writing ministry unpacking the gospel for the heart, proposing that change that doesn't start as deep as the heart may be temporary behavioral modification but isn't truly change. I've applied that message to various dimensions of everyday life, but as I've done so, I have had a concern. I have been bothered that an overspiritualization of the gospel would leave us with a Christian culture that is body ignoring, if not body negative. It has worried me that we would come to see people as disembodied hearts. A gospel for souls that excludes or overlooks bodies is not the gospel of Scripture. The gospel without a theology of the body is a truncated, inadequate gospel. A church that doesn't have a robust gospel theology of the body will be unprepared to meet this generation's philosophical, psychological, sociological, scientific, and media challenges.

We are in a moment when society is asking questions like never before. We cannot go to our social media sites, watch something on Netflix, or read our digital newspaper without hitting this discussion again and again: *Who are we? What do our bodies mean? What does sex mean? What is gender anyway?* This discussion should not make us afraid, and we surely don't have to become part of the confusion, because God has answered these questions for us in his word. The answer is splashed across the pages of Scripture in historical narratives, divine declarations, wisdom principles, and in God's commands and promises. This unsettling moment in culture is a moment of opportunity for us. We can move out in tenderhearted love and grace and speak with surety into the difficulty precisely because God has spoken to us with clarity.

As I mentioned earlier, what you are about to read is a critical book because it gives you a robust theology of your body. No, I don't mean an esoteric, academic, and impersonal handling of the topic. I mean a theology that has the dust of everyday life on it. It's theology that lives where you live and speaks into places where you struggle. It's theology that is bold and clear while being gracious and tenderhearted. It's the kind of theology that ends up not only helping you to understand yourself but also makes you thankful for God, for the wisdom of his word, and for his Son, who shares the majesty and humanity of a body with us.

I am thankful for *What God Has to Say about Our Bodies*, and I am sure when you finish it, you will be too. I can't think of a book that speaks more clearly and more winsomely to our culture's widening dysphoria. My prayer is that it will result not only in clarified thinking but in hearts filled with gratitude and worship for the one who formed our bodies in the garden and will give us new bodies that are form-fit for our final home.

Paul David Tripp
December 3, 2020

Introduction

SOMETIMES WE TEND TO NOTICE our body only when something is wrong with it. A new pain develops. Or we become self-conscious about some aspect or other of our appearance and wish it was different. At other times we can be happily oblivious.

I remember when, as a young schoolchild in biology class, I first saw one of the plastic models of the body's internal workings—the skeleton, the organs, the intestines, and so on—and being both curious and a little repulsed. It was so complex and intricate and yet a bit gross too. It was weird to think that all of that was going on inside me. I didn't want to know much more about it. When some medical issue or other arises, I find out what I need to know to understand what the doctor is telling me. But other than that, I live in generally happy ignorance.

While we tend to focus on our body when it's letting us down, it's easy to ignore it when it comes to spiritual matters. Even the word *spiritual* suggests we're talking about the nonphysical. So when it has come up in conversation that I'm writing a Christian book about the body, many have said, with a quizzical look, something like, "Do you mean the church, and how it is like a body?" That seems to make more initial sense than a book about our actual bodies.

That is why I've written these pages. The first surprise for some of us might be how much the Bible has to say about our body. The second is how the gospel of Jesus Christ is *good news* for our body.

Your body—my body—is not just there, happening to exist. It means something to God. He knows it. He made it. He cares about it. And all that Christ has done in his death and resurrection is not in order for us one day to *escape* our body, but for him one day to *redeem* it. Far from being a spiritual irrelevance, Scripture tells us our body is meaningful—so much of discipleship in the New Testament is spoken of in bodily terms—and it is part of God's eternal plan for us.

PART 1

———

CREATED BODIES

1

Fearfully and Wonderfully Made

The Body and Its Creator

WHENEVER AMERICAN FRIENDS and I engage in friendly discussion about the relative advantages of life in our respective countries (I am British), I tend to feel I'm on the losing side. Sure, life in Britain has lots going for it. We have cream teas, country pubs, moderate weather, chocolate that doesn't taste like wax, and castles that aren't made of plastic. But America has a lot going for it too: optimism, proper lemonade, customer service, better dentistry, and the Grand Canyon. But when it looks like all is lost for dear old Britain, Boxing Day becomes the clincher. In Britain, December 26 is a public holiday, and it's one of my favorites. After all the hype and gastronomic overexertion of Christmas Day, Boxing Day (so called because it was when you'd box up gifts for the poor) is a day to exhale a little. You can rest a bit, pick up and start to enjoy the gifts received the day before, join the cousins, and take the dogs for a walk. In short, you can retain the Christmas vibe but at a more genteel pace. There's lots to do but nothing much that urgently needs to be done.

As I write, it is Boxing Day. Yesterday was Christmas. At church, we heard the apostle John's iconic summary of what happened in Bethlehem so many years ago: "The Word became flesh and dwelt among us" (John 1:14). That's the claim behind Christmas: God became man. For many, the scandal is the claim that there is a God at all. But even more electrifying—both when John first wrote those words and for us today—is the claim about what this God *did*. He became flesh. Theologians call it the "incarnation."

At the center of the Christian faith is the belief that by coming to earth as one of us, Christ could die for our sins, rise to new life, bring us into fellowship with God, and begin the process of putting right all that's gone wrong. But at the center of that claim, tucked away where we don't always see it, is the notion that to become one of us, Jesus had to become *flesh*. To become a human person, he needed to become a human body.

Become a body, not simply don one for a few years. He could, in theory, have turned up as a ready-made thirty-year-old male, prepared to immediately gather his disciples, teach about God's kingdom, and head to the cross. But really becoming one of us took more. To truly become human, Jesus needed to become a fetus in the womb, a baby in a cot, a toddler stumbling about as he learned to walk, a teenager going through puberty, a fully grown man. It wasn't enough to have a body. He needed to truly be one.

Jesus's incarnation is the highest compliment the human body has ever been paid. God not only thought our bodies up and enjoyed putting several billion of them together; he made one for himself. And not just for the Christmas season. The body of Jesus was not like my Christmas pullover, little more than just a festive novelty. No. His body was for life. And for far more than that. After his death he was raised bodily. And after his resurrection he returned to his Father in heaven, also bodily. When he ascended into heaven he didn't ditch his humanity like a space shuttle ditches its booster rockets (to borrow a phrase from N. T. Wright). Becoming human at Christmas was not meant to be reversible. It was permanent. There is now a human body sitting at the right hand of God the Father at the very center of heaven.

Bodies matter. Jesus couldn't become a real human person without one. And we can't hope to enjoy authentic life without one either. That his body matters is proof that mine and yours do too. He became what he valued enough to redeem. He couldn't come for people without coming for their flesh and without coming *as* flesh.

C. S. Lewis sums it up neatly:

> Christianity is almost the only one of the great religions which thoroughly approves of the body—which believes that matter is good, that God Himself once took on a human body, that some kind of body is going to be given to us even in Heaven and is going to be an essential part of our happiness, our beauty and our energy.[1]

This is part of what makes Christianity stand out. It has been common among other religious (and nonreligious) belief systems to demean the body, along with our physicality—to see it as something unspiritual or in need of escaping.

In contrast, the Bible sees our body as a good (if imperfect) creation of God. It is a gift.

We're not used to thinking of our body as a gift. Perhaps one reason is that when we think of our body, we tend to think of the frustrating limitations it places on us. This is true even when it is working well. At the peak of our strength and fitness, our energies and capacities are still finite. As the prophet Isaiah reminds us, "Even youths shall faint and be weary, and young men shall fall exhausted" (Isa. 40:30). We can't be and do all that we would want. We're constrained. Physical life is, by definition, one of being contingent when perhaps we would rather be free. I'm sure this is one of the reasons behind our fascination with the idea of life unconstrainted by our physicality. It is a popular trope in science fiction.

In C. S. Lewis's novel *That Hideous Strength* a secretive scientific lab is attempting to establish a form of human existence that is not dependent on our bodies. It is presented as a great leap forward; our bodies as nothing but an unfortunate constraint that needs to be escaped. As one of the characters puts it:

> In us organic life has produced Mind. It has done its work. After that we want no more of it. We do not want the world any longer furred over with organic life, like what you call the blue mould—all sprouting and budding and breeding and decaying. We must get rid of it. By little and little, of course. Slowly we learn how. Learn to make our brains live with less and less body.[2]

Needless to say, in the novel it is this pursuit that leads to all kinds of evil. And, in any case, most of us wouldn't put it in such a mad-scientist sort of way. But we can nevertheless come to resent the hindrances our body brings, and it is easy for us to see the ways in which our body is a limitation rather than an opportunity.

In the novel (and subsequent movie) *Ready Player One*, humanity in the near future does most of its living in a virtual reality world called the OASIS where we can choose our own appearance. It is not hard to see the appeal:

> In the OASIS the fat could become thin, the ugly could become beautiful, and the shy, extroverted. Or vice versa. You could change your name, age, sex, race, height, weight, voice, hair color, and bone structure. Or you could cease being human altogether, and become an elf, ogre, alien, or any other creature from literature, movies, or mythology.[3]

We're not ditching the body altogether, but we're able to make it take whatever form we could ever want. We exchange what we were born with for something more idealized; something that really feels exactly as we would want ourselves to be.

In one case the body is escaped; in the other, exchanged. But in Christianity neither of those is what we need. The body is intrinsically good, not bad. So it doesn't need to be abandoned or changed into some completely different form. In the words of the apostle Paul, it needs to be redeemed: "We wait eagerly for adoption as sons, the redemption of our bodies" (Rom. 8:23). It is a gift. In a sense, right now, a broken gift in some ways as we'll come to see. But a gift nonetheless.

Handmade

Only one of the presents I got for Christmas yesterday is truly unique. It's not a slight on any of the other gifts, but this one has a property that sets it apart: it was handmade. A friend made me a beautiful, framed, artistic rendering of a favorite Bible verse. To my knowledge it is the only gift I received this year that was not mass-produced. That's not to say it is intrinsically more valuable than the other gifts, but it does make it unusually meaningful.

The Bible shows that our bodies have been very carefully made by God. King David put it famously in the following prayer to God:

> For you formed my inward parts;
>   you knitted me together in my mother's womb.
> I praise you, for I am fearfully and wonderfully made.
>   (Ps. 139:13–14)

God's craftsmanship is not just restricted to David's outside but includes his inward parts. All that he is, both the inner and outer aspects of his being.

David speaks of being made with great care and attention. He has been individually handcrafted. That is not to say his body is perfect. As we'll see later, our body is actually broken; it's not entirely as it was meant to be, and we have all sorts of issues with it. But David can say even of his imperfect and fallen body that it has been "fearfully and wonderfully made."

Fearfully Made

Just think about that language. I think of my friend making that Christmas gift for me. I imagine her lips pursed as she drew the words of the passage and then colored and illustrated them. David says he has been made *fearfully*. Were we to know the full extent of the intricacy of God's workmanship, we would rightly be in awe.

We approach what this means when we see new parents hold their baby for the first time. It looks like it's happening in slow motion as they very carefully pick up and then take care to support the baby in their arms. There is a sense of appropriate fearfulness. They are aware of the sheer preciousness of the little bundle in their arms.

Well, David would say they don't know the half of it. A baby is far more precious and awe-inspiring than we realize. It's not just the delicate body of a baby. Even when we've long outgrown our new-baby cuteness, when we're long past our physical best, and when our body shows all the frailties and limitations of advancing age—whatever stage we're at, we have been fearfully and wonderfully made. We could not begin to measure the value of our body, however it looks and however we feel about it.

Individually Made

There seems to be a trend for artisanal products—coffee shops, bakeries, and the like. When I first noticed this, I didn't know what *artisanal* meant, other than assuming it meant (in the case of the bakery) "misshappen and expensive." But I eventually realized it meant "traditional" and "nonmechanically made." A person made it, not a machine. It may have some imperfections, but even those are proof of authenticity.

Similarly, we human beings are not the product of a factory or the process of copy-and-paste. Our distinctive physical individuality is intended. We have been made by the ultimate artisan. Our God has produced billions of human bodies, but we are not mass-produced. We've each been handcrafted with infinite care. David says we have been "knitted together" in our mother's womb. Now, I've never knitted a stitch of anything in my life, but I've watched others, and it is wonderfully hands-on—each and every stitch individually knit by hand.

Purposefully Made

Being handcrafted means none of us has come about by accident. Our body is not random or arbitrary. I know people who were not planned by their parents—a sensitive issue indeed. They were an "accident," a surprise, and those among them who are aware of their origins can struggle with long-term relational insecurity. But when it comes to God, no one is unplanned. Every one of us is the product of God's deliberate choice. However many people there turn out to be in the whole of human history, not one of them will have been an accident.

The Bible doesn't just affirm that we are all, in some way, the result of God's work, that we have come about because of him. It says much more than that. We're not just the outcome of God's activity; we are the product of God's intention.

Think about it this way. Imagine I am preparing a meal for a group of friends. I have decided, somewhat ambitiously, to cook a meal with several complicated dishes. I am attending to one of these, getting a sauce just right, when I detect the faint smell of smoke. I realize that the meat in the oven is burning. Edible, but burnt. I serve it up anyway. The meal is not going to kill anyone, and parts of it may even be nice, but no one is going to ask for the recipe. Or imagine—and this is less likely—I pull off the entire meal with aplomb. Each component turns out the way I want. It is a success. It may not be perfect in every respect, but nevertheless *this* is what I want my guests to enjoy. In both cases I have produced the meal. In both cases it is the fruit of my labor and work. But only in the second case is the resulting meal what I *intended*.

It is a bit like that with our bodies. It's not that God made them (but didn't particularly care how they turned out). He purposed them. They are what he intended them to be. We can affirm, as

David does, even of these imperfect bodies, that God made them and that he meant to.

Personally Made

All of this means that you have the body God meant for you to have, even when not everything about it is wonderful. It may have any number of problems. It may be a mix of your parents that you didn't want (your dad's eyes and your mother's nose, perhaps, rather than the other way around). But it does mean that God knew what he was doing when he made your body. We can often feel about our body the way we feel when we pick up a hand of cards at the start of a game—why did I have to be dealt this? But in the case of our body, it wasn't random shuffling of the deck or luck of the draw.

The intentionality of our bodies obviously runs counter to how many people think in the Western world today. One article I recently read made the following comment: "Most of us have the bodies we occupy because of luck of the draw."[4] Tellingly, this was simply stated as self-evident fact rather than as an argument. It is easy to just assume our physical origins have no plan or purpose behind them.

If our body is not accidental, it must also therefore not be incidental. If it were merely the product of accidental processes, we could justifiably write it off as having no theological significance. Our body would tell us nothing substantial about who we are. Our sense of self would be found entirely elsewhere, with no necessary reference to our body. But if we have been created, then our body is not some arbitrary lump of matter. It means something. It is not peripheral to our understanding of who we are. For all the difficulties you may have with it, it is the body God wanted you to have. It is a gift.

If this is so, it has some crucial implications for how we are to think about our body.

Being Grateful for Our Body

Our first response to our body should be to give God thanks for it. I am conscious that the words I'm writing are very hard for some to read. They're hard to write. As with so many, my body has been the cause of some very deep pain for me. I know people whose body has even made them think seriously about taking their own life. Our body can lead to horrific suffering—both physical and psychological. The Bible does not deny this and in fact is able to uniquely account for it, as we shall see in due course. Accepting our body as having been fearfully and wonderfully made does not mean we have to pretend everything about it is good.

But however difficult we may find it, the bodily life we have remains a gift from God, one for which we need to be thankful. It is the means he has given for *you* to exist in his world. In the Bible, thankfulness to God is central to our human life, which we see reflected in how Paul describes humanity's turning away: "They did not honor him as God or give thanks to him" (Rom. 1:21). Ingratitude is actually part of the foundation of all sin. Failing to honor God—removing him from his throne and rightful place in our lives—happens alongside and because of our lack of giving thanks to him. Not to give thanks is to forget the goodness of God. It is to neglect the truth that he is, at heart, a God overflowing in kindness and generosity—every good gift comes from him—and that we are fundamentally recipients of his kindness (even with all the complications of life). That Paul couples honoring God with being thankful toward him shows us that unless we see God as fundamentally good, we will find little reason to follow and worship him. Thanksgiving is that foundational.

If thanksgiving is foundational to our Christian life, it should be foundational to how we view our body. We are creatures made by a good and gracious Creator. If even fallen and imperfect bodies are "fearfully and wonderfully made," then we can and should thank our maker for them. It is better to be alive in these bodies than not to be alive at all, even when that life is experienced with great pain.

For those of us who are deeply unhappy with our body, and even resentful of it, the path to a healthy response needs to begin with thanking God. Hard though it may be for us to understand, God meant for us to have our particular body. Your body is a gift.

Being Physically Present

We also need to realize that being embodied means that we are designed to relate to one another physically. Ours is the generation perhaps most in danger of forgetting this. We are able to relate to one another in nonphysical ways. In the last twenty-four hours, I've had online face-to-face conference calls with people from three other countries. Some of the colleagues I work most closely with live on other continents. Two of my best friends live several time zones away. That we can maintain, let alone enjoy, such relationships and friendships shows how much we take today's technology for granted. When some missionary friends of mine had a baby in Thailand, their parents back in the UK could see pictures of their new grandchild within minutes. An earlier generation of missionaries, who could only send pictures via unreliable and slow postal services, would be staggered by how much we can connect. Those living in another country far from you now don't feel much farther away than if they simply lived in another town. We have resources and opportunities that are staggering when we stop and think about them. In some hugely significant ways, technology has triumphed over geography.

But not completely. Alongside these unprecedented opportunities come some very real dangers. Social media means we can be in contact with a huge number of people spread over a potentially huge geographical area. We can message one another and see each other very easily. It can feel like life is hugely relational—all that contact with all those people all the time. But in reality, it is a very incomplete way to relate to others. It gives an illusion of being highly connected but is in fact an insufficient means for cultivating healthy relationships. There is no substitute for physical presence. Hearing people's voices on a call can be wonderful; seeing their faces on a screen even more so. But presence is uniquely meaningful.

Scripture shows us the importance of physical presence in numerous ways. Paul reflects on the time he spent with the Christians in Thessalonica:

> So, being affectionately desirous of you, we were ready to share with you not only the gospel of God but also our own selves, because you had become very dear to us. (1 Thess. 2:8)

Christian ministry for Paul was much more than merely imparting gospel information. He and his colleagues shared their lives with the Thessalonians. His ministry required presence. This is made very plain from the way he continues:

> But since we were torn away from you, brothers, for a short time, in person not in heart, we endeavored the more eagerly and with great desire to see you face to face. (1 Thess. 2:17)

Leaving them was a tearing. Separation was painful. Paul longed for a reunion. Presence with them mattered.

Or consider what John says:

> Though I have much to write to you, I would rather not use paper and ink. Instead I hope to come to you and talk face to face, so that our joy may be complete. (2 John 12)

John's letter is short not because he is lacking things to say to his friends, but because the medium of a letter is ultimately inadequate. "I would rather not use paper and ink." He might say today, "I'd rather not have screen time or online chat." What he wants is to be physically present. That is what will make his joy complete. It's not that there's no joy to be had in online, virtual, or distant relationships, but the joy we can get from them is limited. We need more.

There's a lovely example in Acts of just what physical presence can mean. Paul is in the final stages of his long, arduous journey to Rome:

> And so we came to Rome. And the brothers there, when they heard about us, came as far as the Forum of Appius and Three Taverns to meet us. On seeing them, Paul thanked God and took courage. (Acts 28:14–15)

When the Christians in Rome hear that Paul is finally almost there, they travel out to meet him and accompany him on the final leg of his journey. That might not immediately mean much to us, but bear in mind that the Forum of Appius and Three Taverns are some thirty to forty miles or so from Rome. Traveling that

distance without cars was no small gesture. As far as we know, they
had no urgent business to conduct with Paul. It wasn't a matter of
completing some shared task. They just wanted to be with him.
They wanted Paul to have their company when he finally arrived
at Rome. They wanted to be present.

And what an impact their desire had on Paul. It had been a long
and arduous journey to this point. Yet seeing that these believers
had come all that way just to be with him made a big difference.
He thanked God. It gave him *courage*. Just their presence spoke of
a solidarity that strengthened Paul and gave him a much-needed
boost. Presence really does matter.

Sometimes we approach relationships far too functionally. Sometimes we keep ourselves from others because we're not sure we'll be
much use, especially when it comes to being with those in some
kind of need. Maybe we've never been particularly good with words
and feel sure we won't know what to say. Or we're not good with
making meals or doing practical jobs. But passages like this remind
us of the good that can be done through sheer physical presence.
It probably wouldn't occur to many of us that we could ever be a
spiritual encouragement to someone of the stature of the apostle
Paul. What could we say that he didn't already know? But these
ordinary believers were a genuine help to him just by making the
effort to accompany him for the final day or so of his travel.

A friend of mine pastoring a very difficult congregation once
pointed out a member quietly sitting in the front pew. "He has the
spiritual gift of turning up." This man was evidently very faithful
in his attendance in a church that was hugely volatile. Just seeing
him encouraged his pastor.

Nothing else can do what physical presence does. Other ways
of relating to one another can wonderfully enhance our physical

friendships, but they can never actually replace them. Physical presence matters because we are physical people.

Being Careful Online

Online ways of relating help us overcome some of the limits of our body. We can be in more than one place at once. We can limit what people see of us. We can select the sort of image of ourselves we think best expresses who we want to be. We can log off when we've had enough. But the limits of our physical body are good for us. We're not meant to be everywhere at once. We're not meant to be free from the constraints of being part of a physical community. Being present is a vital part of what it means to be human.

The corollary is also true. If physical presence is a way of honoring our humanity, it is also sadly true that we can all too easily dehumanize those we are not physically around. Something about that form of relating makes it easy to treat people very differently from how we would if we were sitting across from them. This is especially true of our online interactions. When we only experience people as avatars with opinions that rub us the wrong way, we can forget that behind the words is real flesh and blood. They become little more than a position to oppose, so we can find ourselves saying things we would never say if we were sitting across a table from them. Why? Because we're not *with* them. We forget they are people; not just positions we might disagree with. Our priority is how getting these things said will make us feel rather than how hearing might make them feel. Even without realizing it, we can be demeaning and extraordinarily hurtful.

A couple of years ago, the writer and professor Karen Swallow Prior was hit by a bus and very nearly killed. Her recovery was slow and arduous. But she shared some time later that some subsequent attacks she endured online had been more painful than the physical ordeal she had been through.

Our words are powerful. The apostle James likens them to the spark that can ignite an enormous forest fire, and to the deadly poison of an assassin. How much more is this the case when someone is not physically before us. When we are actually with people—even people we don't know well—we naturally and quickly develop the ability to empathize with them. We can see their facial expressions and pick up on their body language. We recognize their sensitivity to things we might be saying. We are aware of what kind of impact our speech is having. If we say something that turns out to be hurtful, we're more likely to realize that and respond accordingly. But when people are hidden behind a screen, all that really seems to matter is making sure we're right and they're wrong. So we can be dismissive of them, or mock what they say, or twist their comments into something we know they wouldn't have meant. We just want to win. They're no longer humans but targets to be bull's-eyed. And all the while, poison is being disseminated, and whole forests are ablaze.

The response is to recognize this and to make every effort never to say something to someone online that we would never say in person. We must treat each word we type as if it was being offered to someone sitting across the table from us. Presence matters. In its absence we need to be all the more careful not to dehumanize.

Being Aware of Appropriate Touch

A recent article highlighted a growing trend in a number of urban areas: professional cuddling services.[5] Paid cuddlers are available for hire by those who feel as though they do not experience adequate physical contact. Some are single; others are happily married. But all feel a sense of being "touch deprived," to use the phrase of a researcher quoted in the article. I've heard it described elsewhere as "skin hunger."

Now some of us might be inclined to roll our eyes. But the fact that such businesses are cropping up is quite significant. There are those in our churches and communities who only very rarely experience healthy touch. Pastor Zack Eswine admits how he "had not imagined . . . how little a widow experiences touch as it is meant to be. Family members live at a distance and visit sporadically. Beyond the pokes of medical people, the elderly often enter a famine of touch as if dwelling in the desert years of their lives."[6]

It is not just the elderly, of course. Professional cuddling agencies report having a wide range of clients. We increasingly find ourselves in a culture that doesn't know how to do physical contact. The slogan of one of these agencies seems to have put its finger on the issue (so to speak): "We're sex obsessed but touch deprived." There is much to this. In Western culture we have collapsed sex and intimacy together to the extent that it is hard for people to conceive of intimacy that is not sexual at its core. So, more and more, we associate touch with being sensual rather than familial.

Churches should provide a remedy by being places where healthy and appropriate touch is encouraged. Paul tells Timothy to treat older men as fathers and older women as mothers (1 Tim. 5:1–2). Churches are meant to be families, so it is entirely appropriate that I greet a church member of an older generation in the way I would greet my own parents.

All of us are to "greet one another with a holy kiss," Paul says on more than one occasion (Rom. 16:16; 2 Cor. 13:12). That will not be the natural form of greeting for every culture in every time, but the principle is clear: we are to greet one another in a physical way that's familial. For most of us in the West, that will involve at least a handshake or perhaps a hug. In some cases (when greeting our spiritual mothers, for example) it might mean a kiss on the cheek. But whatever it is, we must give thought to the appropriate place of touch in our church life.

Boundaries must exist, of course. Not all expressions of physical affection are equal. Paul seems to anticipate that in his language of a "holy" kiss. Zack Eswine contrasts two kinds of physical touch in the New Testament:

> The first is Judas's kiss of Jesus's cheek. This kind of kiss misuses physical touch in order to consume or preserve its own selfish wants, lusts, desires, or agendas (Luke 22:47–48). In contrast the "holy kiss" envisions a way for Christian community to recover in Jesus how human beings were originally meant to touch each other. Physical touch is meant as a holy act. Few of us know in an experiential way what it means to touch or be touched in a sacred way. Profane touch has mentored and broken most of us.[7]

Instead of "profane touch," we are to learn to cultivate in our churches "gospel touch":

> Gospel touch, then, is meant to resemble the touch normatively appropriate between family members. This is your guide. Therefore, abusive, neglectful, presumptuous, or sensual touch has no place in the tender touch of gospel life and ministry.[8]

And what is true of gospel touch should be true of all touch.

The existence of cuddling agencies alerts us to a real issue for many people today, even if these agencies are unlikely to be a plausible solution to the problem. It is hard to imagine that turning touch into a commercial commodity is likely to meet people's genuine needs for meaningful and familial physical contact. The real answer comes when we return to Scripture and recover a healthy biblical view of what it means to have been "fearfully and wonderfully made" as physical creatures.

"The Word became flesh and dwelt among us" (John 1:14). When Jesus stepped into this world as a real, physical human, he reminded us that there is nothing incidental about our physicality. Our bodily life is God's gift to us.

2

Man Looks on the
Outward Appearance

The Body and Our Identity

SOME TIME AGO my friend Andrew Wilson was taking his kids to
the swimming pool on vacation and noticed he was one of only a
minority of men at the pool who didn't have a tattoo. Surrounded
by inked flesh, and having little else to do, he began to note the
various species of tattoo. Most were pictures, words, or names.
The pictures tended to be Eastern-type images of fire and fury,
perhaps an attempt to "project an identity of a dark side and an
understated threat."[1] Many men had tattoos of the names and
birthdays of their children. Others had short phrases. Some were
in English, conveying some motto or philosophy of life. More
were in cooler-looking foreign scripts. All of them—in one way
or another—expressed identity.

When we ink something into our flesh, we make a statement
about how we want to be seen. Some of the swimming-pool men

wanted to be seen as a good father, others as deep or exotic or spiritual. Some wanted to express their loyalty to a particular flag, team, or philosophy. Tattoos are statements. They are physical, painted expressions of how people see themselves, of who they are.

What we hope our body says about us to the outside world is one thing. What it might say to us about who we are is quite another matter.

For some people today, the "real me" is my soul or spirit. The body is simply the lump of matter I am connected to, the outer casing for who I really am. It is the blank canvas on which I can paint my identity once I have discovered it. It is not, in and of itself, part of that identity or a clue to it. It need not determine or constrain who I am. It is the soul that matters. That's where you find the real me. This thinking tends to prioritize the soul over the body. It sees the body as malleable. I can shape it and mold it. I can paint it and adorn it. But what is underneath is much deeper and more immutable.

For others, the body is far more significant. Much of our identity is based on what our body looks like and the extent to which it meets the cultural expectations of what a body should look like. Some today might even wonder if there is such a thing as a "soul" at all—only physical things are real.

Most people may be somewhere in between, or unsure. We might sense that our body means something but not be sure what that something is. Or we might believe that there is much more to us than, say, how we look. But, again, we might not be completely sure what that "much more" consists of.

Our language can reflect some of the confusion. When people let us in on what is really going on in their life, we talk about how they "bared their soul." Or when there has been a terrible tragedy, we might talk about the number of "souls" that have been lost. (Consider how odd it would sound to talk about "the number of bodies" lost in some disaster.) And when it comes to spirituality, we often think about our "inner life" rather than something physical.

The Bible gives us unique insight. To those who tend to see themselves—the "real me"—as the person they feel or believe themselves to be deep down inside, the Bible shows that their body is not incidental to who they are. And to those who have a ton of their identity invested in their body, the Bible shows that there is more to them than how they physically appear to others. Your body is not nothing. Nor is it everything. Is your body *you*? Yes. It is intrinsic to who you are. But it is also not the totality of who you are.

Is My Body *Me*?

In the Bible, our body is not an accessory to who we are; it is *part* of who we are. We can't properly understand who we are apart from our body. Your body is not other than you. It is not just a receptacle for you. It *is* you. In the Bible it's not just that you *have* a body; you *are* a body.

Consider the creation of Adam, the first man:

> When no bush of the field was yet in the land and no small plant of the field had yet sprung up—for the LORD God had not caused it to rain on the land, and there was no man to work the ground, and a mist was going up from the land and was watering the whole face of the ground—then the LORD God formed the man of dust from the ground and breathed into his nostrils the breath of life, and the man became a living creature. (Gen. 2:5–7)

Notice how Adam was made. It was the opposite of how many people today view themselves. God didn't first make a soul called "Adam" and then look around for something physical to put that soul into, as though the soul was the *real* Adam and his body was the equivalent of a Tupperware container to store it in. No. God actually started with matter. He formed a body from the ground, which was then brought to life. As one writer put it, in the Old Testament someone "is an animated body, not an incarnated soul."[2] Your body is not fundamentally a soul that's been shoved into the nearest lump of flesh, as if any old body would do. Carl Trueman sums it up in this way:

> There is no "I" behind or before the body. There is no "us" that exists (logically, let alone chronologically) independently of our flesh and that is then randomly assigned to the bodies we have. Our bodies are an integral part of who we are. And I do not "occupy" my body as I might occupy a house or a space suit or a deck chair at the beach. On the contrary, it is an integral part of me, inseparable from who I am.[3]

Your body is intrinsic to who you are.

Where we use the word *soul* to mean our inner or spiritual life in contrast to the physical body, the Bible typically means something much more all-encompassing. In both Old and New Testaments, the main words we tend to translate as "soul" mean the whole person, not just the nonphysical part of us. It incorporates the body, along with everything that makes us who we are.

So when we read the word *soul* in the Bible, the meaning might be different from how we use the word. Consider the following example from 1 Peter:

> Though you have not seen [Jesus Christ], you love him. Though you do not now see him, you believe in him and rejoice with joy that is inexpressible and filled with glory, obtaining the outcome of your faith, the salvation of your souls. (1 Pet. 1:8–9)

Many of us reading "salvation of your souls" would naturally take it to mean the salvation of the inner, "real" us in contrast to the body. But Peter is actually talking not just about a part of us, but of the whole self, including the body. After all, he has just grounded our entire hope as Christians on the physical resurrection of Jesus (1 Pet. 1:3). The hope is all-encompassing. The whole of who we are—mind, body, spirit (the whole package)—is saved in Christ; it is the salvation of our souls, not in contrast to our bodies but very much including them.

What British theologian Paula Gooder concludes about Paul's use of the word *soul* applies equally well to its use in the rest of the Bible:

> When looking at Paul we cannot and should not assume that when he uses the word "soul" he means something that is fundamentally different from or opposed to the body. . . . [It] is not at all opposed to the body but instead [Paul] incorporates the body into his understanding of what makes us really us. In other words, we cannot be truly who we are apart from our bodies.[4]

Both the main Old Testament and New Testament words for *soul* speak of someone's entire life, the whole person, who someone really is, which very much includes the body.[5]

43

That is not to say there is no distinction between the inner and outer aspects of our lives. There are times when the word *soul* is used in a narrower sense in distinction from the body. Consider these words of Jesus:

> Do not fear those who kill the body but cannot kill the soul. Rather fear him who can destroy both soul and body in hell. (Matt. 10:28)

The distinction here seems to be temporal. The body can be killed in this life, but death is not the end of the person in totality. There is an aspect of them that continues to exist even after they have physically died. There is both warning and comfort in this. The warning is that the eternal punishment of both body and soul by God is to be feared far more than any harm that can be done to us physically in this life. The comfort is that, for followers of Jesus facing even death, nothing can ultimately harm their soul. Physical death is not the worst thing that can happen to us.

So *soul* and *body* can be used distinctively in the Bible but must not be viewed as if they are in opposition. Our body is not separable from who we are.

We see this elsewhere in the Bible. Take these words of Paul to the Corinthians, for example:

> Flee from sexual immorality. Every other sin a person commits is outside the body, but the sexually immoral person sins against his own body. Or do you not know that your body is a temple of the Holy Spirit within you, whom you have from God? You are not your own, for you were bought with a price. So glorify God in your body. (1 Cor. 6:18–20)

These are staggering words, and we'll come back to some of them later in this book. Notice for now how this passage reinforces the importance of the body: Paul uses "you" and "your body" interchangeably here. Look carefully at how he makes his point:

> *Your body* is a temple of the Holy Spirit within *you*, whom you have from God. *You* are not your own, for *you* were bought with a price. So glorify God in *your body.*

"Your body" is another way of talking about the whole of who you are. It is not merely some matter you happen to be responsible for. One group of scholars puts it this way: "Your body is an essential part of *you*, not a vehicle driven by the 'real' you, your mind; nor a mere costume you must don."[6] Paul might well refer to the body as a "tent" (2 Cor. 5:1–5), but even here, the focus is on its temporality and fragility, not on its being something merely external.

This is hugely important. If the body is merely a vehicle or a costume for the real you, then it is the equivalent of property. But we know this can't really be the case. However much we might privilege the mind or soul over the body as the "real" us, we know deep down that the body is an essential part of who we truly are. When people hurt your body, you know that they have not just damaged some of your property; they have violated *you*.[7] What you do to someone's body, you do to a *person*. One book puts it more strongly, with a deeply unpleasant but important scenario: if someone is raped while in a coma, and that person "never finds out and sustains no lasting injuries," it would still be wicked.[8] A *person* is still violated by virtue of the fact that his or her body has been violated. What you do to a body, you do to a person.

We cannot escape our embodied-ness. Alastair Roberts sums it up neatly: "The body isn't just something that clothes the self, but is itself the self."[9]

The Body Is Not Everything

Your body is you. It is not nothing. It's not even just *something*. But neither is it everything. It is not the *totality* of who you are.

In the account of creation, we see that Adam is not *just* a body. God made him but then needed to breathe his own life-giving breath into the matter he had formed for Adam to come alive. On its own, unanimated by God, the body cannot be a living creature. There is no life apart from God's breath. A body without God's life is only a corpse.

It is worth pausing here. Dust was formed into a body, and living breath given into it. Our death is this exact process in reverse. At some point we breathe our last breath. What was breathed into us will one day be breathed out of us. And our body will return to the dust from which humanity was first created. Our humanity is undone. How our life ends reflects how it began.

So your body is not the sum total of who you are. Bodies may be essential, but on their own they are not sufficient. God made them. But we also see that God looks *beyond* them. We see this most clearly in the selection of David as king over Israel in the Old Testament. The first king, Saul, had been rejected by God as king because of his disobedience to God's word (1 Sam. 15:23). It was time for a new king. Saul had effectively been the people's choice—the kind of king they wanted. Now it was time for God's choice—the kind of king that reflected *his* plans and ways. So God directed the prophet Samuel to the household of Jesse; the new king would be one of Jesse's sons. Samuel was to go there and see which of these sons God had selected. Each in turn would be presented to Samuel so that God's choice could be revealed.

It is a classic, celebrated account, as the unexpected youngest son, David, is chosen to be king. But it begs an obvious question: Why did God not just simply announce to Samuel at the beginning who the new king would be? Back when Saul was chosen, the process had been much more straightforward. God had told Samuel that a man would come to him who would be his choice as king, so when Saul then came to Samuel, God told Samuel that Saul was the man he had just said would come. So why didn't God do likewise later and just tell Samuel, "I have chosen David, son of Jesse, to be king over my people"? Why did Samuel need to go through all the hassle and danger of a journey to Bethlehem? And when there, why did he need to have each of Jesse's many sons presented to him rather than just David?

The answer is that this episode is not primarily about the next king, but about God. God looks at people very differently from how we do. When Samuel met the first of Jesse's sons, Eliab, it seemed as though this was the obvious choice as king. He had the right look and stature. It was as if he'd come straight from central casting. He looked the part. And that's the point. God said to Samuel:

Do not look on his appearance or on the height of his stature, because I have rejected him. For the LORD sees not as man sees: man looks on the outward appearance, but the LORD looks on the heart. (1 Sam. 16:7)

God tells Samuel something significant here about humanity. We see one another in a certain way. We look at outward appearance.

Not just that we notice one another's outward appearance, which is natural and understandable, but that we *assess* one another by outward appearance. It may be the most immediate aspect of someone, but we tend to treat it as the most significant aspect. We size people up. We assess how they look and make our determination about them primarily on that basis. We know there's more to people than how they look, but we nevertheless resort to making appearance what shapes our estimation of them.

Samuel is a case in point. One look at Eliab, and it seemed obvious. We're told exactly what Samuel thought: *Surely this is God's anointed man!* We would have done the same thing. But God is different. His way of looking is radically different from ours. Where we tend to begin and end with outward appearance, God goes much further beyond. He sees into what is inward and much less prominent. He looks on the heart. He sees not just how we appear but who we truly are, outside *and* in.

God's perspective is reinforced by the choice he eventually makes from Jesse's household. Just as it at first seemed completely obvious whom God would choose—dashing, tall Eliab—so too it looked equally obvious whom God was not going to choose. So obvious, in fact, that Jesse hadn't even bothered to send for David, instead leaving him out in the fields looking after the sheep. Given the strapping alternatives, there's no way David was even under consideration. Best to leave him out of the picture. Yet he was the man God chose. We're told a little about David's appearance— "ruddy" with "beautiful eyes" and "handsome" (1 Sam. 16:12). Not exactly horrible to look at, granted, but also not exactly the kind of rugged person you'd cast as king either. David might not have been what we'd think of as the right *image* of a king, but he was the right *person*.

Jesse's sons were paraded before Samuel—and before us—for this very reason. We need to see how our usual way of seeing, though natural and understandable, to some extent, is not sufficient. We might tend to start with outward appearance, but we mustn't stop there. Your physical appearance before the world around you, with its bodily particularities, is not what ultimately sums you up. You are more than your externals. You are more than your body.

We all need to hear this, whether or not we (and others) are pleased with our outward bodily appearance. There are a host of reasons we might not like the body we have. We'll look at why that is and some of what lies behind that later in this book. But for now, we need to know that in God's estimation, we are much more than our appearance. Your body, in all its glory and limitations, is you. But it is not the totality of you. Realizing this will help you have a healthy view of yourself. It will also help you have a healthy view of others. Looking only at the physical gives us a very limited and incomplete picture of someone.

The Body Is Not Nothing

If one mistake is to think about the body as if it is the sum total of who we are, another, as touched on earlier, is to think of it as if it has no bearing at all on who we are, or as though the essence of who we are is entirely independent of our body. This latter way of thinking seems to be more and more prevalent in the West today.

Think about the hit movie *Avatar*. On its release in 2009 it quickly became the highest-grossing movie ever made, with a slew of sequels immediately announced to follow in due course. Set 150 years in the future, it is the story of humans on a distant moon, Pandora, inhabited by a race known as the Na'vi—tall, blue-skinned humanoids. In order to infiltrate this race, humans use specially created hybrid bodies called "avatars."

While there is much that can account for the record-breaking success of this movie—the innovative special effects, for example— it is surely no coincidence that it suggests a view of personhood in which one's body is entirely exchangeable. The main character, Sully, is in fact paraplegic. Yet via his avatar, he is able to enjoy the use of fully working limbs. Underlying the movie is the assumption that your body is little more than a costume. You can inhabit a completely different body—even that of different humanoid species—without it changing who you are.[10] Your personal identity may be expressed through your body, but it is in no way dependent on it. You could just as easily be you in another body entirely.

Avatar expresses what is a common way of thinking today. Increasingly, it is not to the body we look to get a sense of who we truly are. The "real" us is not discovered by looking at the body but to the soul within. As one writer puts it, "the 'real me' is a soul tightly and hermetically sealed within my body" and it is this that accounts for "what makes me uniquely me."[11] The soul, as popularly understood, carries far more significance than the body. Theologian Tom Wright puts it this way:

> The great controlling myth of our time has been the belief that within each one of us there is a real, inner, private "self," long buried beneath layers of socialization and attempted cultural and religious control, and needing to be rediscovered if we are to live authentic lives.[12]

I just saw a trailer for a movie tipped for Oscar greatness. A key moment seems to be when an older man says to the younger main character, "At some point you've gotta decide for yourself who you're gonna be. Don't let nobody make that decision for you." Wright estimates that "perhaps half the novels written today, perhaps two-thirds of the Hollywood movies, have this as their subtext."[13]

Needless to say, defining ourselves by an inner sense of who we are then becomes the basis for our ethical thinking. Whatever this true self wants and desires is self-justifying. We have to be authentic, and this quest legitimizes virtually any kind of behavior. The longings and yearnings we find deep within ourselves have to be granted in order for us to be true to who we are.

So we see a growing priority given to the soul, the inner self. The body is merely incidental to our identity. What really counts is what we find within. It is not hard to see how this kind of thinking has had a huge influence on the Western church in general. Where earlier generations of Christians esteemed sacrifice and service of others as the highest kind of virtue, we are more likely today to hear church leaders speak of the need to be true to ourselves. In our culture, the hero today is not the person who risks his body for the sake of others, but the person who lays aside anything and anyone for the sake of being authentic. We most esteem not self-sacrifice, but self-expression. It is not uncommon now to hear of even leading Christians justify abandoning biblical ethics on the basis of having to be "true to who I really am." But "who I really am" can't be considered without reference to my body. Carl Trueman puts it this way:

> [My body] is perhaps the foundational piece of evidence that, were I to claim that I am, for example, Attila the Hun or Nancy Pelosi, I would be talking nonsense, with my body as Exhibit A in the case for the prosecution. It is not simply instrumental to my identity; my identity is inseparable from it. To downgrade

it to a mere incidental, or to set the real me in opposition to it, is a recipe for chaos.[14]

The corollary to Western culture's view of the body not being defining in any way is that what we do with it does not really affect us. If the "real you" is the inner self you understand yourself to be, then what your body does is not ultimately meaningful. It is just the body, not really you.

Perhaps we see this thinking most clearly with how people increasingly view sex as simply a physical act with no significance beyond that. "It was just physical; it didn't mean anything"—we are used to hearing this sort of justification. But if we are our bodies, then what we do with them really does mean something. What our body does, *we* are doing.

Paul shows us this in 1 Corinthians. Evidently, many in Corinth had bought into the mindset that what is done with the body is not spiritually significant. In the case of some, it led them to believe that sex was spiritually beneath them, and so Paul had to actually tell them to not abstain from sex within marriage (1 Cor. 7:2–4). Others instead seemed to think that if the body is not spiritually significant, then it didn't matter who they had sex with, and so they were engaging in forms of sexual sin, including having sex with prostitutes. Paul's words to them are very instructive:

Flee from sexual immorality. Every other sin a person commits is outside the body, but the sexually immoral person sins against his own body. (1 Cor. 6:18)

There is a sense in which sexual sin is unlike any other sin. It is a sin "against" our "own body." There are many ways we abuse and degrade our bodies. But something more deep and lasting is happening when we engage in sexual sin: we are sinning against our very selves. As we have seen, Paul uses "your body" and "you" interchangeably in this part of his letter. Sex is a sin against the body because it is a sin against the whole person, and it is a sin against the whole person because God has designed sex to *involve* the whole person. We cannot avoid that reality. In the right context, it is a glorious truth. Sex is a way by which we give ourselves fully to someone else. It can never truly be just a physical act. As Australian theologian and pastor Michael Jensen has written, "Saying 'It's only sex' is basically admitting that you are something else apart from your body, and giving in to the fantasy that you can cordon off yourself from your body in some way."[15] Paul would agree. Sex is, properly speaking, unavoidably and profoundly *personal*. Sexual sin is not just a misuse of your body but a violation of your whole self. No wonder Paul tells us not just to avoid it but to flee it. The repercussions of engaging in it are enormous. It does something deep to who we are.

Different Christians may have differing views over whether tattoos are good, bad, or neutral. But the fact that there has been such a dramatic increase is significant. Perhaps for many, it is a sign that our flesh needs to be "branded" in order to show that it is truly ours, that, un-inked, it is unable to tell the story of who we really are. For others it might simply be an attempt to flaunt what they believe to be their physical attraction or prowess. So tattoos can be a sign that we're thinking of our body both too little and too much. Only the Bible will help us have the right view. When it comes to our identity, our body is not everything. But neither is it nothing.

3

Male and Female He Created Them

The Body and Biological Sex

IN LATE 2015—which now feels like light-years ago—*Vanity Fair* featured on its cover the former Olympic champion Bruce Jenner. Jenner had begun to identify as a woman and posed provocatively under the caption, "Call me Caitlyn." Jenner had been identifying as transgender for some time, but the public journey from Bruce to Caitlyn had been completed. It was a moment that seemed to signal, more than anything else, that the transgender revolution had officially arrived.

In the short years since then, of course, so much has changed that it feels as though *Vanity Fair*'s cover is old news. It wouldn't shock us today. Many other celebrities have publicly identified as transgender and shaped the conversation in new ways. Western society has changed dramatically in how it thinks and speaks about sex and gender. What seemed prevailing cultural wisdom even only a decade ago has now been turned on its head. There are new protocols, terms to use, words to avoid, and attitudes to signal—all often enforced aggressively.

For those who've lived through the change, it can easily feel bewildering. For those who came of age during it, this change can feel intuitive and normal. But for all of us, whether we feel like cultural immigrants or cultural natives, how we think about gender deeply reflects what we think of our body. All of us—let's be frank—are deeply aware of our own sexual organs. The question is, do they have any meaning? Do they have anything to tell us about who we are? Do they shape how we experience the world around us?

Even within a highly secular culture, there is not one fixed mindset on the answers to those questions. While most seem happy to allow transgender people to identify as they choose, there is enormous contention over the issue of whether biology makes *any* difference to our understanding of gender. Many advocating for trans rights will say it doesn't; *all* that matters is who people deeply believe themselves to be. A trans woman (someone who grew up biologically male now identifying as a woman), they would strenuously say, is no different from someone who grew up biologically female—"trans women are women."

But a number of other groups in the secular world are not so sure. Some trans people themselves believe there is still a difference between a biological male and a transgender man, or between a biological female and a transgender woman. Some feminists have also questioned this aspect of transgender ideology. Feminism has traditionally been predicated on the belief that the story of human history is one of biological men oppressing biological women and that transgender women cannot fully enter into the experience of full womanhood if they have not themselves had to grow up biologically female. There are also a number of LGB voices raising similar questions. The experience of being gay and lesbian is based on having attractions to people of the same biological sex but not necessarily of the same gender identity. So they want to argue that their identity is actually based on the understanding that there is a biological difference between male and female.

Christian Scripture provides us with unique insight and clarity. It shows us that our biology *is* meaningful. Our experience of growing up male or female is part of what makes us *us*. It also shows us that there are nonbiological aspects to being men and women that are real and meaningful as well—though these are often misidentified both within the culture and within the church.

Being embodied is a fundamental part of what makes us human. You cannot fully be you without a body. You cannot fully be you without *your* body. It is a gift. It is part of your calling. Your way of being you includes your body and your sex. Our starting point needs to be the Bible's starting point—the account of creation, and especially God's creation of humanity:

Then God said, "Let us make man in our image, after our likeness. And let them have dominion over the fish of the sea and over the birds of the heavens and over the livestock and over all the earth and over every creeping thing that creeps on the earth."

So God created man in his own image,
in the image of God he created him;
male and female he created them.

And God blessed them. And God said to them, "Be fruitful and multiply and fill the earth and subdue it, and have dominion over the fish of the sea and over the birds of the heavens and over every living thing that moves on the earth." (Gen. 1:26–28)

This is where we humans make our first appearance in the Bible: God declaring his intent to make us and then creating us in his image. It is also the first time there is mention of our biological sex. We are not just made as people; we're made male and female. Right from this outset this aspect of our humanness is highlighted. So what do we learn about being male and female here?

Maleness and Femaleness Are Embodied
Maleness and femaleness are physically grounded, not psychologically determined. When Genesis 1:27 talks about us being made male and female, it is talking about us being *physically* made as such. All through Genesis 1 God was physically forming and filling his creation. Immediately before the creation of humanity God made physical creatures to populate the land, sea, and sky. When he announced his intention to make human beings, and to make them male and female, he was clearly not talking about a concept of maleness and femaleness somehow unrelated to our physical bodies. As he physically made us, he physically made us male and female.

There is more to be said on God's design, of course. Much more. We'll see that being male and female isn't only about our biology. There is more to it than that. But there is not less. A definition of maleness and femaleness that makes no reference to our physical bodies cannot be biblical.

Whatever the biological reality, there are many who feel a deep and profound sense of unease with their own biological sex, an experience called "gender dysphoria." This experience is real and worthy of our understanding and care. Those who face it need support and sympathy and not glib responses or (even worse) demeaning comments. As we'll come to see later, Christians, of all people, have the most reason to be compassionate when it comes to this struggle. But Genesis 1 shows us that however complex our experience may be (and I suspect it is not entirely straightforward for the vast majority of us), we mustn't make that experience the arbiter of what is true about us. Our gender identity is not something we search for in our feelings; it is something we find in our body.

The fact that God created us male and female is also reflected in Genesis 2:

> Therefore a man shall leave his father and his mother and hold fast to his wife, and they shall become one flesh. And the man and his wife were both naked and were not ashamed. (Gen. 2:24–25)

We notice that the language has shifted from "male" and "female" (which are not unique to humanity) to "man" and "woman" (which are unique to humanity). Rob Smith notes:

> The clear implication of this move from "male" and "female" (in Genesis 1) to "man" and "woman" (in Genesis 2), an implication everywhere confirmed as the biblical narrative unfolds, is that *a person's biological sex reveals and determines both their objective gender* (*what* gender they, in fact, are) *and certain key gender roles* (should they be taken up). That is, human males grow into men (and potentially husbands and fathers) and human females grow into women (and potentially wives and mothers). Indeed it is this set of binary connections that makes human marriage possible.[1]

Maleness and Femaleness Are a Binary

In Genesis 1, humanity is described as "male and female." Two sexes are mentioned; biologically, gender is presented in Genesis 1 as binary. We all have different experiences of sex and gender, of course. Some will feel male, say, but perhaps not fully male (in whatever way they consider maleness). As we've seen already and will think about in more detail later on, some experience gender dysphoria—perhaps being biologically male but feeling female. Some may feel somewhere in between. But whatever our experience might seem to be telling us, we need to evaluate it in the light of what we see here in Scripture rather than trying to change Scripture to fit how we feel.

The account in Genesis presents two biological sexes, not any other number. It does not present sex as a spectrum or a continuum along which people are expected to be evenly spread.[2] But what of those who are born seemingly neither male nor female? What should we make of this? Such people clearly exist and will most often go through significant hardship as a result. The presence of intersex people represents a biological aberration rather than a biological norm or additional third biological sex. But there is much more to be said.

As we have already seen, all of us, irrespective of any biological challenges we may face, of any kind, have been fearfully and wonderfully made. There are no exceptions. As we'll see in more detail in a later chapter, our bodies are all fallen; we all encounter a measure of bodily brokenness. But that does not take away from the care with which God has made us.

We also need to affirm that all people are made in God's image. "In the image of God he created him; male and female he created them" does not mean that someone who doesn't seem to be either male or female is not made in God's image. Genesis 1 does not restrict the image of God only to those whose biological sex is obvious at birth.

Some might respond by saying that while Genesis 1 talks about biological sex being binary, it represents the world before sin distorted everything in Genesis 3. In other words, Genesis 1 is about how God made us *then*, not about how he makes us *now*. But we need to see that the same language of being made male and female is repeated in the Bible even after the fall of humanity into sin in Genesis 3. Consider these words just a couple of chapters after the fall:

> This is the book of the generations of Adam. When God created man, he made him in the likeness of God. Male and female he created them, and he blessed them and named them Man when they were created. (Gen. 5:1–2)

These verses reassert the ongoing significance of how God had created humanity to a post–Genesis 3 world.

Leaping much further ahead, we see the same truth on the lips of Jesus during his earthly ministry:

> Pharisees came up to him and tested him by asking, "Is it lawful to divorce one's wife for any cause?" He answered, "Have you not read that he who created them from the beginning made them male and female, and said, 'Therefore a man shall leave his father and his mother and hold fast to his wife, and the two shall become one flesh'?" (Matt. 19:3–5)

Jesus was asked about divorce. He answered by talking about how marriage is a solemn union. But to talk about marriage, he had to go back not just to the first marriage in the Bible (in Genesis 2), but to the creation of humankind as male and female (in Genesis 1, as we've seen). He not only reaffirms the existence of the male/female binary, but in doing so shows us that it remains the basis on which marriage exists. Because God has made us male and female, there is such a thing as marriage—not just in Genesis 2 with Adam and Eve, but ever since then and continuing today. Marriage is grounded on the union of two sexually different people. So however much sin has spoiled our understanding and experience of being male and female, it hasn't obliterated the distinction between the two sexes. We human beings do not come in an indeterminate number of sexes. We are still made in God's image as male and female. We can see from this that intersex is a condition that comes after the fall. It is not part of the original design God had for humanity in creation. It is an identifiable deviation from the male-female pattern rather than constituting a third sex.

Significantly, in the very passage where Jesus reaffirms the ongoing significance of the male/female binary, he goes on to say something which acknowledges that our physical experience of this might not always be straightforward:

> For there are eunuchs who have been so from birth, and there are eunuchs who have been made eunuchs by men, and there are eunuchs who have made themselves eunuchs for the sake of the kingdom of heaven. (Matt. 19:12)

Jesus is talking about eunuchs and mentions that some "have been so from birth." Eunuchs were typically men who had been castrated for some special vocational reason (such as serving in the inner circle of the emperor). But some are born eunuchs, not simply made that way by others. In other words, they were born not having every biological feature we expect a baby boy to have. Certainly there are other manifestations of intersex bodies, but here, Jesus is talking about a male who was born anatomically "incomplete." But it nevertheless highlights the reality of complexity in our physical experience of being male or female. The duality exists, but that doesn't necessarily mean that everything is straightforward, any more than the presence of biological irregularities doesn't mean that God hasn't made us male and female.[3] Rob Smith concludes, "Scripture resists diluting the sex/gender binary, even though some do not fit neatly into it."[4]

An (imperfect) analogy might help. Color-blind people find it either hard or impossible to distinguish between green and red. Color-blindness is not uncommon—you may in fact experience it. And, thankfully, there are lots of work-arounds to keep it from being too much of a hindrance to daily life. But it is nevertheless a reality for many. But just because some struggle to distinguish red from green doesn't mean that the colors red and green do not actually exist. They clearly do. They are objective realities. That some confuse one for the other does not change that. In fact, when we drive, our lives depend on the fact that these two colors really do exist and are not subjectively determined. Yet the fact that these colors exist doesn't mean that there is no confusion or difficulty for anyone. There is.

This short text in Matthew 19 does not answer every question we have about the phenomenon of intersex people—this was not the focus of what Jesus was teaching about in this passage—but it shows us perhaps what we most need to know. To those whose biological reality is painful and confusing, Jesus gets it. He sees it. He expects this to be the case for some people in a broken and fallen world. The biological complexity some might have to face is, as we'll see, part of the bodily brokenness that all of us have to reckon with in one way or another. For every single one of us, our body is imperfect and causes us some amount of suffering. Such suffering varies hugely from person to person, but no one should feel somehow in a category of their own. Your experience may be very different from that of other people. It may seem that no one else, however much they try, truly gets it. That may be true. But Jesus sees all and knows all. He has lived as a human on this earth and suffered the extremities of physical pain. He is not "unable to sympathize with our weaknesses, but . . . in every respect has been tempted as we are, yet without sin" (Heb. 4:15).

The one who asserts this male/female duality has unique understanding of what each of us has to face in life.

Maleness and Femaleness Are Essential for Image Bearing

There is an important way in which we humans are like every other creature God has made—he is the Creator and we are his creation. We depend on him and are subject to him. We tend to think too highly of ourselves and quickly feel that we might know a thing or two more than God does about how to run the universe, but at the end of the day, we and the universe fully belong to him and not he to us.

But there is also an important way in which we are quite unlike all other creatures. The text in Genesis 1 has already shown us. We are made in his image:

> Then God said, "Let us make man in our image, after our likeness. And let them have dominion over the fish of the sea and over the birds of the heavens and over the livestock and over all the earth and over every creeping thing that creeps on the earth."

So God created man in his own image,
in the image of God he created him;
male and female he created them. (Gen. 1:26–27)

The uniqueness of humanity was anticipated before our arrival, just in the way our creation is announced. Up until this point God created by summoning the various elements of the universe into existence: "Let there be light," "Let the land produce," etc. But at this point God announces his intention to make us before the actual act of creating. Not "Let there be . . ." but "Let us make . . ."

We immediately see what accounts for this special introduction to humanity. We are to be made in God's image. Everything else in creation reflects something of God's glory in a general sense, but humanity alone is described as being created in God's image. Our correspondence to God is on a different level. We glorify God in a unique and more direct way. We *image* him, which is not only informative; it is breathtaking. No wonder the description of the actual moment of creation is set out in poetic form. This is artistry. And that we are made in God's image is highlighted again twice in 1:27. Image bearing is our vocation as people.

Being made in God's image means that we have the capacity and calling to reflect God to the world, to represent him to his creation, which is confirmed by the work God gave his newly created people to do:

God blessed them. And God said to them, "Be fruitful and multiply and fill the earth and subdue it, and have dominion over the fish of the sea and over the birds of the heavens and over every living thing that moves on the earth." (Gen. 1:28)

In other words, humanity was to be as God to the creation, to tend, develop, and care for it on his behalf, as he would. There is dominion, to be sure, not as an end in itself but as a means of expressing the Creator's own intention for his world, to "reflect, continue, and to extend God's own creative rule."[5] Putting it another way, "God made us for the exalted purpose of representing him."[6]

But as our image bearing is stressed, so too is our sexual differentiation as male and female. This is no accident. Our sexual difference is bound up with how we are to image God.

There are all sorts of things that distinguish us from one another as human beings. We can have very different temperaments, personality types, and ethnic and cultural backgrounds. We have different tastes, skills, and capacities. But these don't define us in quite the same way or to the same extent. It is our sexual difference as male and female that gets star billing. As Alastair Roberts notes, "Sexual difference is the one difference that is prominent in the creation narrative."[7] We will not fully understand what it means to be made male and female without understanding how foundational it is to how we image and reflect God.

We humans, of course, are not unique in being made male and female. I write this from a room in a friend's house with two cats in almost permanent attendance, one male and one female. The natural world is full of creatures that display this sexual difference. So what is significant is not the *fact* of our being male and female, but what it *means* for us. It reflects something that animal sexuality is unable to.

Ray Ortlund puts it this way: "Both male and female display the glory of God with equal brilliance."[8] We are clearly talking about something far more than reproduction. Ortlund goes on to say, "Animal reproduction is *assumed*, but human sexuality is *celebrated.*"[9] There is something not merely functional about our differentiated sexuality, but something dazzling. We men and women are equal, yes. But there is more than that.

It is not that we each comprise half of what it means to be made in God's image, and the combination of a male and female together makes up one whole image. No. Each individual human being, male and female, is fully made in God's image. Instead, what Genesis 1 is showing us is that male and female need each other to better image God. There is something about the interplay between the two that enriches us. Tim Keller has put it this way:

> In Genesis 1 you see pairs of different but complementary things made to work together: heaven and earth, sea and land, even God and humanity. It is part of the brilliance of God's creation that diverse, unlike things are made to unite and create dynamic wholes which generate more and more life and beauty through their relationships. As N. T. Wright points out, the creation and uniting of male and female at the end of Genesis 2 is the climax of all this.
>
> That means that male and female have unique, non-interchangeable glories—they each see and do things that the other cannot. Sex was created by God to be a way to mingle these strengths and glories within a lifelong covenant of marriage. Marriage is the most intense (though not the only) place where this reunion of male and female takes place in human life. Male and female reshape, learn from, and work together.[10]

We need each other. Each sex alone constitutes the image of God. But that image is more fully reflected by the interplay between male and female.

Reflecting God as male and female may sound rather alien to much of Western society, but there is a level on which we instinctively recognize it. We sense that there are certain contexts where having only one sex present is diminishing in some way. We're aware, for example, of what some secular leadership spaces might lack if there are only men present. It is not just a question of representation or fairness. The interplay of our respective glories enriches all of us. Being male and female is designed to help us be better at being people. It is not just a matter of biology, but of theology; not just about the multiplication of humanity, but the fuller imaging of God.

4

God Formed the Man

The Body and Gender

I'VE RECENTLY BEEN SETTING UP a new home and therefore spending more time than I would ever choose trying to assemble furniture. If I never see another Allen key for the rest of my life, I will be a very happy man. Needless to say, the results have not been uniformly impressive. The best appraisal I can give myself at the end of a sweaty day is, "That'll just have to do." And when you're talking about a bed you'll be spending around a third of your life lying on, "that'll have to do" is not great. I already seem to have done my back in as a result of it. With God it is very different, which is great news for all concerned, not least us.

There is a rhythm to the account of creation in Genesis 1. The work takes place over six days, with a repeated refrain coming at the end of those days: "God saw that it was good." God is evidently not inattentive to what he is making. He doesn't start one aspect of creation and then turn his attention to the next project. He finishes each act, steps back (as it were) and appraises it. As he assesses each day's work of creation, he can be fully pleased with the outcome. So again and again we read, "It was good," "It was good," "It was good."

That is, until we turn up. At the end of the day when God has made humanity in his image, male and female, he says something different: "It was very good" (Gen. 1:31). The difference male and female image bearers makes to his creation is to lift it from "good" to "very good." Needless to say, it is not a track record we maintain through the rest of the Bible; but the fact remains, there is a deep fundamental very-goodness to the way God has designed us to be, and our being made as men and women is at the heart of it.

Of course, whenever we talk about God's design for men and women, significant questions rush to the front of our minds. What exactly does it *mean* to be a man, or to be a woman? What should it look like? Or feel like? These are not abstract questions. Each of us has some story of how we experience our own sex. Each of us has some sort of instinct about what we are supposed to measure up to and whether we have reached it or remain woefully short of it. Much of how we feel about ourselves, along with our social confidence and our mental health, can ride on this. It matters.

And it is confusing. It feels as though there are so many potential and available answers to those questions, and they don't cohere. What a man or woman should be like not only varies from culture to culture but enormously within cultures, from one generation to the next and one region to the next—even from one locker room to the next. I'm not sure I know how to answer all those questions, but I find that two simple observations about the Bible give me the basic coordinates I need to start thinking about it.

The first observation is that the vast majority of what God has to say, he says to us as men and women without distinction. It is obvious to point out, but despite the best marketing strategies from publishers, there is not one Bible for men and another for women. The same Bible is given to both. And all the words within it are for both men and women to read. Even the parts addressed to men are still meant to be read by women, and those addressed to women by men. So whatever differences there may be between us, we must not exaggerate them. We are not different species. It is not the case (to use the language of a hugely popular book from several years ago) that men are from Mars and women from Venus. However much we may mystify, surprise, or delight one another, we are far, far more alike than we are different.

In fact, the very first interaction between a man and a woman in the Bible highlights this very point. We've already seen the repeated refrain in Genesis 1 of "It was good," "It was good," and finally, "It was very good." But even more jarring than the addition of the word *very* is the addition of the word *not* in Genesis 2. In this close-up account of the creation of Adam and Eve, Adam is at this point on his own. And this time, as God steps back he declares this not good:

> Then the LORD God said, "It is not good that the man should be alone; I will make him a helper fit for him." (Gen. 2:18)[1]

The man on his own is inadequate and insufficient. He needs an appropriate other. "Fit for him" here also carries the sense of "corresponding to him," someone who will be his match.

But God doesn't then immediately create the first woman.[2] Instead, he brings out various creatures before Adam for him to name. And by naming, he doesn't mean giving each single creature its own personal name; he means taxonomy—giving each kind of creature its appropriate name. So this involves carefully examining the nature of each species and kind so that he can give it a proper designation. Doing this only brings home to him that each creature is distinct from him. The conclusion? "But for Adam there was not found a helper fit for him" (Gen. 2:20). The not-goodness of his original situation has not changed. On the positive side, Adam now knows what to call everything; but on the negative side, he is still without a necessary counterpart.

So *then* God makes the first woman. Having had every creaturely form of "not like him" paraded in front of him, Adam can at last now truly appreciate a creature who *is* like him. So when Eve arrives, it is her *likeness* to him that lights up Adam:

This at last is bone of my bones
    and flesh of my flesh;
she shall be called Woman,
    because she was taken out of Man. (Gen. 2:23)

What first leaps out at Adam is not all the things that are *different* between Eve and him but the very fundamental way in which she is *like* him. There are differences. He's not oblivious to that—evidenced by the one-flesh union they quickly enter into. But more fundamental than the obvious differences between men and women is the more fundamental likeness. Our human commonality precedes our sexual difference.

So our shared likeness as human beings is seen in that the vast majority of what God says to us in the Bible, he says to us as men and women without distinction. We're not directed into separate rooms; we share the same holy Scripture. There may be ways in which we think or behave differently, but this should not be stressed at the expense of how alike we are.

The second observation is that while is it essential to know that the vast majority of what God says is said to us without distinction, it is not true of *everything* God says. So while we have obvious differences of biology, the fact that at times we need to hear slightly different words from God indicates these differences extend beyond biology. It does not seem to be the case that, biology aside, men and women are indistinguishable from one another.

How we identify what these deeper, nonbiological differences are requires great care. With an issue so sensitive and far-reaching, we want to make every effort to go only as far as the Bible goes—no further and no less.

Not Saying What the Bible Doesn't Say

A while ago a friend told me of a Christian homeschooling textbook that purported to teach what the Bible says about what it means to be a man or a woman. Various traits for both were presented, along with some accompanying Bible verses as justification. One of the assertions about women was that they are to be dainty. But with this assertion, there was no Bible verse to back it up—presumably because no such Bible verse exists. And yet this trait was still listed, because those behind the textbook evidently thought daintiness was the sort of thing the Bible *should* say characterizes a woman.

It is very easy for Christians, often without realizing it, to go further than the Bible says. We each have our own deep sense of what constitutes true masculinity and femininity, and we can all too easily assume that sense has come from the Bible, especially if we're holding it in contrast to what a wider, secular culture around us might be saying. But what seems obvious and instinctive to us about the nature of men and women might reflect our own cultural prejudices more than what the Bible actually says.

So we must be careful about saying that all men or all women should be this way or that way, or that men should be interested in these things and women in those things. More often than not, we will not find these views in the Bible.

Not Exaggerating What the Bible Does Say

We want to say what the Bible says; we also want to say it only to the *extent* that the Bible says it. Sometimes we can take a genuinely biblical idea and run with it in a way that the Bible itself never does. What we end up saying might not be contradicted by Scripture and may well be consistent with one aspect of what the Bible says, while not actually being biblical. The Pharisees give us a number of examples of how easily this happens. They rightly took the Old Testament law seriously. But they often mistook their application of God's law for the law itself. So those who didn't obey the law *in the exact way that they did* were regarded as disobedient.

I suspect the same often happens when it comes to discussions of what Christian men and women are meant to do or be like. Principles found in Scripture get applied in prescriptive ways that exceed the scope of the original text, and anyone who disagrees is accused not of disagreeing with the application but with the Bible itself. I've seen this sort of thing numerous times, particularly in the conservative churches from which I have come. I think of one church where, in mixed prayer meetings, women were discouraged from praying at the beginning because it would discourage men from taking the lead in prayer. I can imagine (just about) this being well-intentioned to start with (perhaps seeking to apply 1 Timothy 2:8—"I desire then that in every place the men should pray"?), but by the time I encountered this practice, it had already been hardened into a rule about what men and women should do: men should always be first to pray in a mixed gathering; women should always hold back and wait until the men have prayed first.

So those of us (I include myself) who believe that Scripture teaches that only certain qualified men should serve as pastors or elders in the church need to be careful not to then take this teaching and start applying it to contexts the Bible never speaks to, such as women leading in certain secular contexts. Or those who take the Bible's teaching to husbands and wives and then end up prescribing from this which spouse should be doing which tasks in the modern home.

These examples are from conservative churches, because those are the ones I have belonged to. I am sure the same thing happens in any kind of church. We take a biblical command or principle and determine exactly how it should be applied and equate how we apply it with what the Bible actually says.

Not Saying Less than the Bible Says

Saying what the Bible doesn't say or overextending what it does say are both forms of adding to Scripture. But we must be equally careful not to subtract from Scripture. And if (in my experience) adding tends to happen more in conservative churches (perhaps an unintended consequence of wanting to take the detail of Scripture seriously, then (also in my experience) subtracting tends to happen more in less conservative churches (perhaps an unintended consequence of not wanting to be bound by rules and conventions that aren't biblical). Either way, all of us are in danger of both.

The fact is, it is clear from Scripture that differences between men and women are not just physiological. And while we mustn't overdefine what these differences are, neither must we deny they exist at all. This is especially important given that it is increasingly common to think that being equal must mean being the same in every respect—that equality cannot properly exist where there is any kind of difference. But the Bible challenges this way of thinking. Our very difference is what makes each gender distinctly glorious. We can't simply hope to swap out a man for a woman, or a woman for a man, and assume it will make no difference. C. S. Lewis puts it in this way (here referring to sex as biological sex rather than as intercourse):

> The kind of equality which implies that the equals are inter-changeable (like counters or identical machines) is, among humans, a legal fiction. It may be a useful legal fiction. But in church we turn our backs on fictions. One of the ends for which sex was created was to symbolize to us the hidden things of God. One of the functions of human marriage is to express the nature of the union between Christ and the Church. We have no authority to take the living and semitive figures which God has painted on the canvas of our nature and shift them about as if they were geometrical figures.[3]

Each gender therefore needs and complements the other. Each helps the other in the task of imaging God. We need each other. This is how God has designed us. When we attempt to make men and women somehow interchangeable, we are subtracting not just from God's word but from his blessing.

So we mustn't add to, inappropriately extend, or subtract from what the Bible says. We need to take great care in how we think and speak about gender distinctions. That said, what should we say? To begin to answer, it may be helpful to look at the question,

How do the nonphysical differences between men and women relate to the physical differences?

How Do the Nonphysical Differences between Men and Women Relate to the Physical Differences?

In C. S. Lewis's science fiction novel *Perelandra*, Dr. Ransom is on the planet Venus and at one point witnesses an angelic celebration. He realizes that some of the angels seem to be masculine and some feminine. We're told that Ransom "found that he could point to no single feature wherein the difference resided, yet it was impossible to ignore."[4] There was something unmissable and yet also indefinable about this masculinity and femininity. Some of us may relate: we know masculinity and femininity exist, we recognize them when we see them, but we struggle to put our finger on exactly what each consists of.

In his book *The Meaning of Marriage*, Tim Keller makes a similar point:

> It is my experience that it is nearly impossible to come up with a single, detailed, and very specific set of "manly" or "womanly" characteristics that fits every temperament and culture. Rather than defining "masculinity" and "femininity" (a traditional approach) or denying and suppressing them (a secular approach), I propose that within each Christian community you watch for and appreciate the inevitable differences that will appear between male and female in your particular generation, culture, people, and place.[5]

This means that true, biblical masculinity and true, biblical femininity are, respectively, simply what naturally emerges when men and women grow in Christ. Biblically speaking, masculinity is what long-term sanctification produces in Christian men and femininity what long-term sanctification produces in women.

This must certainly be true; whatever else manhood and womanhood are, they can't be less than, or different from, godliness in a man or a woman. We can often recognize real masculinity and femininity when we see it, even if we don't necessarily feel able to pin such things down.

Writer and teacher Jen Wilkin suggests that our physical differences go some way to explaining our nonphysical differences. For example, she says, the greater physical size and strength of most men compared to most women significantly shapes how each sex sees the world.[6] Women, she suggests, will more likely be conscious of physical vulnerability in a way that won't generally be the case with as many men, and as a result women are more likely to be attuned to and sympathetic toward vulnerability in others.

I was recently glancing at a discussion on Facebook about transgenderism and noticed that someone—not a Christian, by all accounts—made a similar point. The issue was whether transgender women (biological males identifying as female) could fully enter into the experience of womanhood without having had to encounter the world as a biological female, and this commenter (a woman) said, "In my experience men finally 'get it' when they become elderly. You have no clue what it's like to live in a world where half the population can beat you to a pulp." Entering into older age and beginning to experience a measure of physical vulnerability can help men understand something of what many women have experienced in the course of their whole lives.

This principle—that many of the observable differences between men and women have their origins in our physical differences—makes a lot of sense. Our body, soul, and spirit are deeply connected, as we've seen. It would certainly make sense that our bodily encounter with the world would shape how we each instinctively think, perceive, and behave. It would also make sense that the physical commonalities we share as a biological sex lead to general and observable differences between men and women that are nevertheless not absolute and which will vary from culture to culture.

Some of these differences may be reflected in biblical passages addressed specifically to men or women. We need to be careful not to read more into such texts than may be there, especially by generalizing from something that may be particular. But it strikes me that in a number of places we may be getting some indirect glimpses into what some of our nonphysical differences look like.

In his instructions to Timothy about church life in Ephesus, Paul directs the following instructions to men:

I desire then that in every place the men should pray, lifting holy hands without anger or quarreling. (1 Tim. 2:8)

Paul is directing this call to pray specifically to men. This is not to suggest that Paul doesn't want the women in the church to similarly lift up holy hands in prayer. The rest of the Bible makes abundantly clear that prayer is not a privilege reserved only for men. All Christians are to be people of prayer. But for some reason Paul felt that this needed to be said to the men in particular.

It seems that Paul's words were triggered by particular behavior he'd learned about in the Christian circles he was writing to. Among the men, prayer was either being neglected or it was being practiced alongside ongoing enmity between them. Paul's response is clear:

he wants the men to lift holy hands in prayer. The focus is not so much on the hands being lifted as on them being pure. We'll see at a later point that the Bible shows us a range of postures that were used in prayer—we'll need to come back and think about that. But the point here is less about the posture than the attitude.

But though there is clearly specific behavior Paul is responding to, we also see that it has wider application. Paul hints at this by saying he wants men to be praying "in every place." This goes far beyond what the guys are up to in Ephesus; the directive extends to men everywhere (and, by implication, in every time). This is not just for them there; it is for us too.

This being so, it may reflect something more generally true of men than women. Men are generally more likely to need to hear the admonition to pray than women. It is not that women don't need the same level of encouragement to pray—they do. The issue instead is that perhaps men, overall, are more likely to be quarrelsome—not universally (all men, without exception), absolutely (all men to the same extent, with no variation), or exclusively (only men, as if women couldn't be quarrelsome), but generally, typically. And if this is the case, then it makes sense of what Paul is calling men to do in response. If there is a tendency for men to be quarrelsome, then calling them to be men of prayer instead is not arbitrary. Rather than wrestle one another in conflict, they are to wrestle God in prayer (like Epaphras, in Colossians 4:12). Better to have "hands raised in prayer to God, not raised in clenched fists towards one another."[7] Inasmuch as men sense this trait within them, it is something that can be channeled in a healthy way and put to spiritual use.

The same may be true of what Paul then says to women in the next verses:

> Women should adorn themselves in respectable apparel, with modesty and self-control, not with braided hair and gold or pearls or costly attire, but with what is proper for women who profess godliness—with good works. (1 Tim. 2:9–10)

Again, we can assume Paul's exhortation is prompted by particular behavior among his readers that he had become aware of. He is correcting a real issue in a real place. But (also again) the fact that this comes in a letter in which the aim is to show "how one ought to behave in the household of God" (1 Tim. 3:15), we can assume it is not *only* about them but has wider significance beyond Ephesus at that time. If I am correct, we might expect to see another correlation between what Paul is steering them away from and what he is steering them to. The issue seems to be ostentatious dress. Not that Paul is discouraging effort in appearance; he's discouraging effort that is deliberately attention seeking. This tendency isn't entirely absent among men, and again Paul is not arguing against personal grooming or taking care in one's appearance; he is arguing against ostentation.

Surely there is significance in that Paul's instruction is directed toward women and not toward men. Just as not only men can be quarrelsome, so too not only women can be vain about appearance. But just as it is telling that Paul directed men in particular not to be quarrelsome, it is likely telling that here it is women he directs not to be ostentatious. I think we can legitimately infer from this that ostentation might be more of an issue among women in general than among men.

And just as Paul, observing a particular trait among men, directed them to channel that trait in a more spiritually constructive direction, so too he does the same here. If there is a tendency to draw the attention of others anywhere, it's better to draw it toward God through good works than toward self through ostentatious appearance.

These texts were both prompted by Paul's observing and redirecting negative traits. But he observes positive traits too. Writing to the Christians in Thessalonica, Paul reminds them of how he had ministered when he had been with them in person:

> We were gentle among you, like a nursing mother taking care of her own children. (1 Thess. 2:7)

Paul often likens gospel ministry to the work of a parent. Here he specifically likens it to the work of a mother nursing small children. There was a warmth and tenderness in his ministry that brings to his mind how a mother cares for such a young child.

We mustn't read into the maternal imagery more than is clearly there, but it is interesting that Paul should especially associate these traits with women nursing babies. He expects such care to be present among mothers. However typically they may be so, they are clearly not exclusively so, as here we find Paul himself embodying the very same qualities in his apostolic ministry. This sort of tenderness is not uniformly going to be present in all mothers without exception, nor should men shy away from being characterized by it (or Paul would not be drawing attention to his own example of it). Gentleness, with all that it involves, is part of the fruit of the Holy Spirit that all believers are called to bear (Gal. 5:22–23). If it is true that it is more commonly found in women (or at least in nursing mothers), it is not meant to be found only there.

This surely is the point. Inasmuch as there may be traits (positive and negative) that are generally true of men and women, we must not be hard and fast about it. Such traits (again, inasmuch as they exist) are not going to be characteristic of any sex absolutely, universally, or exclusively. They may be typical, but they will also be unevenly present and shared with the other sex as well. If, say, gentleness is more typical of women, it isn't equally true of all women to the same extent. And some men are gentler than some women. This does not mean that such men are in any way lacking in their masculinity; it simply reflects that we manifest the ninefold fruit of the Holy Spirit in differing proportions, between the sexes and within them. God has not called women to bear half the fruit of the Spirit and men the other half. All of us are to be marked by all that comprises this fruit—love, joy, peace, patience, kindness, goodness, gentleness, faithfulness and self-control. We celebrate these wherever we see them, and we never stigmatize any who bear some of them in surprising measure. Being more manly will never mean being less spiritual. Sam Andreades puts it this way:

> Gender comes in specialties. Specialties are things we all might do sometimes, but the specialist focuses on especially doing them. We may do many things for each other that are the same, but the gender magic happens when we lean into the asymmetries. Just as, physically, both males and females need both androgen and estrogen hormones, and it is the relative amounts that differ in the sexes, so the gender distinctives are things that both men and women may be able to do, and *do* do, but when done as specialties to one another, they propel relationship.[8]

So the differences that exist are not absolute, as though the things men can do *only* men can do, and the things women can do *no man* could ever do. Yet there are some general ways in which men and women are distinct from each other while at the same time being very much alike. We are not meant to be interchangeable, so that all one can do, the other must also do in exactly the same way. It is not always helpful to compare one with another, as though we are pitted against each other in a zero-sum competition.[9]

As with many things, G. K. Chesterton hits the nail on the head in this short poem:

> If I set the sun beside the moon,
> And if I set the land beside the sea,
> And if I set the town beside the country,
> And if I set the man beside the woman,
> I suppose some fool would talk about one being better.[10]

PART 2

———————

BROKEN BODIES

5

Subjected to Futility

The Body, Affliction, and Shame

CERTAIN THINGS CHANGE when you turn forty:

- The world starts becoming too loud.
- You get excited about going to bed.
- You still get badly hurt, but now you don't have a good story to account for it.

The fact is, when you're under forty and injured, it's usually because you were doing something exciting—jumping out of a plane, or wrestling a shark. If you're over forty, your most serious injuries come just from sleeping.

A couple of years ago, I was staying in an unfamiliar hotel and woke the first morning with hot, searing pain through my shoulder. It felt like I'd just been mortally stabbed by a Ringwraith from *Lord of the Rings*.[1] It was agony. I called reception, and they sent the hospital doctor to see me. In the end, he had to inject some painkillers—using the largest needle I had ever seen not being used on an elephant. All this, and what had I done? He told me I'd slept on my shoulder "the wrong way." One of the most painful things I'd ever done to myself, and the cause was lying in bed sleeping.

Our bodies have been fearfully and wonderfully made. But they also cause us pain. Because we live in a created world, our bodies are a gift. But because we live in a fallen world, they might not be the gift we would have wanted. Our bodies are broken. The same Bible that shows them to be God's handiwork also describes them as "earthen vessels" or "jars of clay" (2 Cor. 4:7).

This simple metaphor might tell us more than we realize at first. Jars of clay are not just humble (compared to jars of cut glass, for example). They're weak and fragile. They're not robust, but easily cracked. Invariably, in this world, they break. The Bible shows us something of why this is. Writing to the Christians in Rome, Paul says:

> The creation was subjected to futility, not willingly, but because of him who subjected it, in hope that the creation itself will be set free from its bondage to corruption and obtain the freedom of the glory of the children of God. (Rom. 8:20–21)

Creation has been subjected to frustration. Think about that. The good world God so carefully made has been put out of joint in some way. It no longer runs smoothly. Something has happened that means it doesn't work properly as it was originally intended to. It sputters and falters. The world is not always a wonderful place to be. Quite apart from the suffering caused by us, the natural world itself can seem vicious and cruel. A glance just at today's world headlines includes stories of disease and natural disasters wreaking havoc in many places. This frustration to which it has been subjected is not its natural, happy state.

This explains something of our perplexity at the sufferings we experience. We have only ever lived in a world where these sorts of difficulties occur. We've never known anything else. And yet we cannot reconcile ourselves to it. Our gut reaction is that these things should not be so. This sense is hard to explain other than as a memory trace of a different world where such things do not happen, a homing device for the world as it was intended to be.

The physical world that has been subjected to frustration includes our bodies. They are part of the natural order to which we belong. They are made of the same stuff that has been put out of joint. And so they, too, do not work as they were originally meant to. They get sick. Sometimes they stay sick. They break and deform. They age and decay. And all of them, at some point, die. This, too, is evidence of the futility that now marks much of creation.

Paul is clear that this frustration and futility have been imposed on creation. It is not creation's own choice. It comes "because of him who subjected it," namely, God. If we zoom out from Romans 8 to the wider narrative of the Bible, we can see how this happened. When the first people sinned in Genesis 3, they disrupted their relationship with God and with one another. They also triggered a disruption in their relationship with the natural world. "Cursed is the ground because of you," God told them (Gen. 3:17). The brokenness of this world is a consequence of the brokenness of our relationship with God. That *creation* doesn't work as it was originally intended to, and as we sense it should, is a reminder that *we* don't relate to God as we were originally intended to.

In the classic movie *E.T. the Extra-Terrestrial* the lovable alien forms connections with some living things close to him. He revives some dying flowers, and from that point on they reflect E.T.'s own health. When he falls sick and dies, we see the flowers finally withering with their petals falling off. But one of the signs that E.T.'s death is not the end is when the flowers unexpectedly and suddenly spring back to life. To the onlooking boy Elliott, it can only mean one thing. If the flowers have burst back into life, then E.T. must have as well.

Similarly, we are to see the nature of the physical world as a sign of humanity's own standing before God. Nature is still glorious—the sun is setting beautifully behind a nearby hill as I write this—yet it is also deeply painful. We human beings still reflect something of the dignity of having been made in the image of God yet know ourselves to be deeply sinful and broken in the depths of our heart. Our broken glory is reflected in nature's broken glory.

Paul is also clear that this broken glory is not the end of the story. Strangely, God has subjected the world to futility "in hope." There is a positive, not just punitive, purpose here. Something good is anticipated in this sad situation. The hope is that "the creation itself will be set free from its bondage to corruption and obtain the freedom of the glory of the children of God." God is going to establish children for himself, children who reflect something of his glory. And something at least of that glory will consist in how they have been freed from the bondage that is the natural lot of sinful human beings. Paul is describing how God will bring people to himself through Christ, freed and forgiven—released to be the people they were always created to be as children of their Creator.

And creation itself is somehow going to share in this freedom too. Just as human sin dragged creation down with it, so too human liberation will lift creation up. As people find their freedom, so too will creation. And that includes our bodies, as we shall see. Paul goes on to talk about the prospect of "the redemption of our bodies" (Rom. 8:24). Ultimately the pains and struggles we experience in our bodies are not a sign that our bodies have no value but that God hasn't finished with them yet.

All that is to come. Redemption—bodily redemption—awaits. Frustration is not the end of the story. But it is the part of the story we find ourselves in now. And we cannot escape it. As long as we live in this fallen world as fallen people, we will experience some kind of bodily brokenness. It will always be unmistakable that we are jars of clay. We see this brokenness in a number of ways.

Infirmity and Sickness

In his moving memoir Michael J. Fox describes the first moment his body showed signs of the Parkinson's disease that was to increasingly ravage it. He was lying in bed in a hotel room and noticed the little finger on his left hand wouldn't stop twitching:

> That morning my brain was serving notice: it had initiated divorce from my mind. Efforts to contest or reconcile would be futile. No grounds were given, and the petition was irrevocable. My brain was demanding, and incrementally seizing, custody of my body, beginning with the outermost pinkie on my left hand.[2]

It was the beginning of the process that over the years would see Fox losing more and more control of his body.

An estimated 53 million suffer from Parkinson's, including 1 percent of those over sixty. Fox's experience, sadly, is not at all unique.

I think of a cherished member of my church who, like Fox, was first diagnosed with Parkinson's while still a relatively young man. As the decades wore on, it became increasingly hard for him to be mobile, and he spent many of his last years at home and largely confined to bed, his body wracked with pain.

Parkinson's is, of course, just one of the many ways our bodies can be afflicted. All of us know people with chronic or severe health problems. In any given week at our church, we seem to pray for someone with cancer, or about to undergo serious surgery, or who is bereaved. Of my close friends, I can think of someone who suffers from severe Crohn's disease, one awaiting surgery for brain cancer, and another undergoing chemo for pancreatic cancer. I have good friends who have lost children through miscarriage and sickness. These are just among my close friends. I'm sure it's no different among yours.

Some years ago I was at a church prayer meeting where we were told that a much-loved church member had just received a nasty diagnosis from her doctor. I remember walking back home that night wondering how I would cope if I was ever diagnosed with a serious medical condition. That night I woke several times with intense abdominal pain, which continued for a day or two until I went to the doctor, was sent to the hospital, and eventually diagnosed with Crohn's disease. Over the next two years I was admitted to the hospital about eight times, each time for a few days. I've had major surgery and several smaller procedures. I've spent more nights than I care to remember in the hospital and have a disfigured abdomen to show for it. And my health experience is way, way better than that of many people I can think of. I think of my experience of Crohn's as more of a shot across the bow than a definitive answer to the question I had after that prayer meeting. I may have to cope with a much harder diagnosis one day.

I know someone who has had debilitating health problems her entire life. I can well imagine her temptation to resent the body that has caused her so much pain. It may well be hard for someone in that situation to hear talk about our bodies being "fearfully and wonderfully made" (Ps. 139:14). Such language is not wrong or misleading (it's in the Bible!), but on its own it is incomplete. They *are* fearfully and wonderfully made. They are also deeply broken. And for some, the pain is unbearable.

There will always be some who are tempted to think that an individual's illness or suffering is the sign or consequence of some particular sin. This kind of thinking was around in Jesus's day. When the disciples encountered a man who had been blind from birth, they asked Jesus, "Rabbi, who sinned, this man or his parents, that he was born blind?" (John 9:2).

It can be a natural way to think. Hardwired into most of us is some sense that we all get what we deserve. So it is easy to apply that mindset to sickness and infirmity and wonder if the suffering isn't some sort of payback for sins. But Jesus is unequivocal in his response: "It was not that this man sinned, or his parents" (John 9:3). We're not to extrapolate from someone's suffering what they might have done to deserve it. It doesn't work like that. The main connection between suffering and sin is at a general, humanity-wide level rather than at an individual level. It is not that one person's suffering is a sign of his or her sin, but that *anyone's* suffering is a sign of *everyone's* sin.

And being a Christian doesn't exempt us from this. Being made right with God does not instantly de-frustrate the part of creation that we call our body. Suffering is still to be expected. The idea that Christians are shielded from sickness and infirmity is a wicked denial of what the Bible says.

Scripture gives us plenty of examples of God's people experiencing sickness and suffering. When Timothy experiences recurring ailments with his stomach, Paul doesn't tell him God will deliver him from this sickness if he hangs in there and prays hard enough. No, Paul prescribes a commonsense solution: "Use a little wine for the sake of your stomach" (1 Tim. 5:23). God is able to heal, and there are times when he chooses to. We see those in the Bible too. But he doesn't promise to. There are also times when he enables us to develop a cure for a particular sickness. But this too is not always the case. And even when it does happen, it is no guarantee we won't end up afflicted by something else.

Body Shame

Infirmity is not the only problem we encounter with our body. It is possible to experience minimal health problems and yet still find that our body causes us deep and lasting grief. Bodies are not just subject to infirmity; they can cause us shame.

For some, the shame comes from appearance. We might feel as though there is something deeply wrong with some aspect of how we look, convinced that in certain key ways we do not measure up. Some can even feel disgust with the entirety of their body.

These feelings seem to be on the rise in the West. In 2014, 54 percent of women described themselves as "unhappy with their body," and 80 percent said that looking in the mirror "made them feel bad." These numbers are significantly higher than in previous years. I am sure there are many contributing factors, but one is surely that, more and more, we are being presented with unrealistic standards of beauty. Models and actors are subjected to training and dietary regimens that are often unsustainable, hugely expensive, and extreme. And even then, images are cropped, airbrushed, and recolored so that the final image we end up seeing on a giant poster may not actually be *anyone's* actual body but a weird hybrid of one or more people and a whole lot of digital editing.

The trouble is, the end result is presented to us as representing the bodily perfection to which we should all aspire. It may not be how the actual model or actor looks, or at least how he or she looked for long, but we're left thinking that the model is what human beings are meant to look like. Author Matthew Lee Anderson notes that earlier generations were not exposed to such outlandish standards of beauty.[3] The best-looking person you'd see back then was likely in a newspaper or magazine, or someone you knew in real life. But it was a *real* person. Today we all collude in upholding an expectation of beauty that is virtually fantastical. No wonder we view our bodies as increasingly flawed. We're not comparing them to the best of our species but to the best of our species' imagination.

Whatever the cause, body shame is a serious issue for all of us, men and women alike. The impact around us is more and more evident. Over the past couple of years or so, as it's come up in conversation that I'm thinking through what the Bible says about our bodies, many people have opened up about their own experiences of body shame. I'd always known that body shame isn't uncommon, but I hadn't anticipated just how widespread it is. It may actually be abnormal *not* to struggle with it in some way.

Shelby, a good buddy of mine, is in his mid-thirties, married, and has a great job where he can use his creative skills as a writer and speaker. I'd always assumed Shelby is a confident guy. He is good at what he does and really likable. But then he told me how he struggles:

Here's the thing—I'm short. I've always been that way, and from a very early age, I can remember being made fun of for being below average when it came to height. Naturally, I joked about this on a regular basis to get laughs and protect myself from getting injured by the cruelty of people's words, should they be inclined to get laughs themselves at my expense. I would just try to beat them to the punch.

On one occasion, as a student, Shelby was hanging out with some friends. Two of the girls said they were about to take off and asked if any of the guys wanted to walk them back to campus:

> I quickly volunteered to walk them both back, and after doing so in what I could only assume was an attempt to be funny, my friend Anne looked at Kirsten and said, "Does he *count*?"
>
> And because I was regularly willing to shell out short jokes about myself, Anne probably felt comfortable that night doing so, thinking it would be funny and really no big deal. What Anne didn't know, however, is that I would carry that little three-word question with me for years to come. It would deeply wound me and define the heart of my struggle in life as a person, a man, a friend, a romantic option for a girl, a missionary, and even a child of God.

Sharing the incident with me even decades later, Shelby choked up. These words had truly haunted him ever since, hanging over his life as a constant charge against him. Those words made him believe his height was forever proof that he is diminished as a man, as a person, and even as a Christian. But then words do that. And words about people's bodies can particularly do that, because our bodies are so often things we have little control over. When we pass a verdict on someone's body, we are passing a verdict on something about who that person is that he didn't necessarily choose and can't necessarily change. No wonder Shelby was so deeply scarred by what they said. Such wounds can easily stay with us for the rest of our lives.

One of the curious features of body shame is how varied it can be. Someone struggling with one kind can be baffled that someone else would struggle with another kind. I've known some guys who don't ever want to take their shirts off at the beach or the pool because they're overweight. I've known others who won't do the same thing because they're skinny. Those in the former category can sometimes wonder how someone could feel shamed about being thin. But that's how these things work. One thin friend shared that when he was growing up, he was always told men were meant to be powerfully built. Being scrawny was a sign you weren't a real man.

The nature of body shame is that there's no one variety. We all seem vulnerable, especially in our formative years, to hearing or seeing things that trigger a deep sense of shame about the way we look.

The Bible speaks to bodily shame. When Adam and Eve turned against God in the garden of Eden, it wasn't just their relationship with God that was spoiled. Their relationship to each other and to themselves was also affected. The first thing to happen when they each sinned against God was that they became physically self-conscious:

> Then the eyes of both were opened, and they knew that they were naked. And they sewed fig leaves together and made themselves loincloths. (Gen. 3:7)

Previously they had been naked and unashamed (Gen. 2:25). It would never have occurred to them that nakedness was anything to be ashamed about. Afterward, in Genesis 3, everything had changed. They were still together as a couple and would remain so. They would continue their one-flesh relationship (Gen. 4:1). But they no longer felt completely safe around each other. A deep instinct had arisen in each of them that they needed to cover up, to self-protect. Exposure had become something to fear.

We're now, it seems, hardwired to feel a sense of vulnerability when it comes to our body. We fear not just literal nakedness but a more general sense of being uncovered. We don't want to be seen. We fear the shame it could bring. This being so, we need to be careful not to make our own words the cause of someone else's physical shame. In the case of my friend Shelby, it was just three syllables: "Does he count?" That can be all it takes.

A few years ago I was flying to Sydney, and the plane flew high above a vast bushfire. The scale could only really be appreciated from the height of 40,000 feet. Horizon to horizon was scorched. I couldn't begin to calculate how many thousands of acres were affected, and yet all this havoc was likely started by a single spark. Just like what can happen with our words:

> How great a forest is set ablaze by such a small fire! And the tongue is a fire, a world of unrighteousness. The tongue is set among our members, staining the whole body, setting on fire the entire course of life and set on fire by hell. (James 3:5–6)

There is another reason why these sorts of comments are so serious. When we disparage people because of the way they are physically, we are not just disparaging them; we are disparaging the

God in whose image they have been carefully made. A person may be the intended target of a cruel joke or comment, but God is the one who is ultimately insulted. We are asserting that he has made something substandard. We insult not only what he has made but also him for making it.

I think of another friend who has struggled with an eating disorder over the years. At its worst he had been dangerously thin. He explained that part of what had been going on was that, because of some earlier abuse he had experienced, he had come to view his body as shameful and so felt a compulsion to make it as thin as possible. Food became not something to enjoy but merely calories and micro-nutrients to quantify. Thankfully he has begun to think about himself differently and to achieve a much healthier weight.

These are obviously highly complex issues. The examples I've given happen to be men. Most of my pastoral encounters are with men rather than women. And given that many people today still think body shame is predominantly an issue for women, it might be helpful to consider these male examples. The effects of the fall touch all of us in varying ways. All of us experience something of the shame of Adam and Eve in Genesis 3. All of us feel the need for covering. All of us have some degree of self-consciousness. In many cases, the brokenness is not so much the body itself, but how our experience has taught us to view the body. The brokenness of our culture, our family, our friendship circle, our own distorted view of who we are meant to be and what we are meant to look like—all these things interact and contribute to our sense of shame.

Underlying all of it is our collective and individual turning away from God. Whatever relief and help we may be able to find from other places, we ultimately need to come back to God. As we shall soon see, the answer to all bodily brokenness is the broken body of Jesus.

The Body Is Dead Because of Sin

The Body, Sin, and Death

FOR A COUNTRY THAT INVENTED a lot of sports, England is not very good at winning them these days. Take our favorite sport as a nation—football (or as you Americans call it, soccer). England has not won a football World Cup since 1966, a period of time closer to the sinking of the *Titanic* than to today. But that doesn't stop us English living as though 1966 was just a couple of years ago and as if our next victory is therefore just around the corner. Bobby Moore was the man who captained the nation to victory. His is the name forever remembered. He was the one to receive the coveted trophy from the hands of Queen Elizabeth.

That exact moment was not as glorious for him as we might think. As Moore walked up the steps at Wembley Stadium to receive the World Cup from the queen, he became aware of something that evidently filled him with dread. She was wearing pristine white gloves. He was caked in mud, hands included. He was going to have to shake her hand with his. So when you watch footage of him walking up the steps, you can see him frantically wiping his hands on his clothes trying to get the dirt off.

As we've begun to think about the brokenness of our body, we have had to think about the fact that many of us feel a sense of shame about it. We feel as though it is in some way blemished, unclean, spoiled. We've seen that this dilemma is as old as human sin. Our estrangement from God has left us all with a sense of needing to cover up and protect ourselves. But shame does not just come about because of how we look. It can also be caused directly by sin—our own and other people's. Shame can come because of what we have done with our body. None of us has used our body exactly in the way God intended. This is how Jesus gave his own executive summary of God's law:

> "You shall love the Lord your God with all your heart and with all your soul and with all your mind and with all your strength." . . . "You shall love your neighbor as yourself." There is no other commandment greater than these. (Mark 12:30–31)

This is what we were designed for: loving God with all that we are, and loving our neighbor as ourselves. So this is, therefore, what our body is intended for. It is meant to be a means by which we live in this love of God and others. The two go together, of course. Failing to love others is by definition a failure to love the God who made them. They might be our neighbor, but they are his handiwork. And a failure to love God always leads to a lack of neighbor love, for God is the one who shows us what true love looks like. Apart from him, we can never fully know what love truly is and means.

But it is immediately evident that this has not been the story of our body. Our body has not been used 24/7 to love God and others. It has been the site and means of our own sinful agenda. We've walked away when we should have been present to help. We've physically lashed out when we should have walked away. We've written and said words designed to crush someone else and exalt ourselves. Our physicality has become so deeply entwined with our sinfulness. And at times it catches up with us and we feel deep shame. The apostle Paul knew this well:

> So I find it to be a law that when I want to do right, evil lies close at hand. For I delight in the law of God, in my inner being, but I see in my members another law waging war against the law of my mind and making me captive to the law of sin that dwells in my members. Wretched man that I am! Who will deliver me from this body of death? (Rom. 7:21–24)

Even when our intentions are worthy, we still find ourselves veering off into sin. We find ourselves to be like old shopping carts with mangled wheels: when we try to push them forward, they end up lurching sideways.

Notice how bodily Paul's language is here. He twice refers to his "members"—his body. This is where sin so often is seen to operate. We might know in theory (in our head, at least) what we should be doing, but within us physically we see a deep loyalty to sin. It can feel as though there is a force within that isn't actually on our side. Paul ends up exclaiming, "Who will deliver me from this body of death?" because that is what it feels like it has become. So much sin and devastation has taken place in and through our bodies. It has become ground zero for our experience of our own sinfulness.

This might account for how Paul often uses the word *flesh* (*sarx* in the Greek) as a substitute or shorthand for our sinful nature and moral weaknesses.[1] One of the most dramatic examples comes in Galatians:

> I say, walk by the Spirit, and you will not gratify the desires of the flesh. For the desires of the flesh are against the Spirit, and the desires of the Spirit are against the flesh, for these are opposed to each other, to keep you from doing the things you want to do. (Gal. 5:16–17)

Such strong language can be easily misunderstood. We might think that sin is only a bodily issue. Or we might think that the body has become intrinsically bad because of sin. Both of these are mistaken. We have already seen that our bodies, even though fallen, are still intrinsically good. As we have already seen, King David—himself no stranger to the sinful ways our bodies end up being used—could still refer to his fallen body as having been "fearfully and wonderfully made" (Ps. 139:14).

On other occasions, Paul also uses the word *flesh* in a neutral way, just as we would ordinarily use it—to describe our physical matter:

> Not all flesh is the same, but there is one kind for humans, another for animals, another for birds, and another for fish. (1 Cor. 15:39)

Here Paul is simply referring to the meat on the bones of different creatures and observing the natural differences. He does not mean anything negative. He is simply describing our fleshly variety as creatures.

So when Paul does use *flesh* in the negative sense, we mustn't assume that it reflects everything Paul thought about our bodies. If anything, it serves to underline the sheer tragedy of how our God-given bodies have become so used for sin.

Bodily sin can take any number of forms. We are quite adept at finding misuses for virtually any part of the body:

> For while we were living in the flesh, our sinful passions, aroused by the law, were at work in our members to bear fruit for death. (Rom. 7:5)

Paul is talking about the explosive effect the law of God can have on sinful men and women. Once again, "living in the flesh" is shorthand for life before and without Christ. In such a state, the law of God ended up actually accelerating our sinful passions, giving them something to react to and work against. What is important for us to note though is that these passions "were at work in our members." *Members* here simply means the parts of our bodies. It is as though there was no aspect of our body that our sinful nature couldn't find some use for.

Just earlier in the same letter Paul had written:

> Let not sin therefore reign in your mortal body, to make you obey its passions. Do not present your members to sin as instruments for unrighteousness. (Rom. 6:12–13)

Our natural state is one in which sin does reign in our "mortal body." He draws attention to our mortality precisely because (as we shall see) it is the ultimate proof and consequence of our sinfulness. That our bodies die illustrates the fact that sin has reigned in them.

Paul also commands us not to "present [our] members to sin as instruments for unrighteousness." Again, he is simply describing what is the default setting for every human being apart from Christ: we manage to find ways of using each part of the body for our own unrighteous agenda. This is not to say that before we knew Christ we only ever used our body for explicit evil. It is simply saying that our native instinct is to use all that we have at our disposal for our own, spiritually oblivious purposes. When Paul sums up the universality of human sinfulness with a string of Old Testament quotations, it is revealing how much bodily language is used:

> "Their throat is an open grave;
>   they use their tongues to deceive."
> "The venom of asps is under their lips."
>   "Their mouth is full of curses and bitterness."
> "Their feet are swift to shed blood."
>   (Rom. 3:13–15)

No part of the body has been left out. Every aspect of our physicality has in some way been pressed into service of sin. It is why, as we shall see, we must now as Christians be diligent in consecrating every part of our body to Christ.

However, lest we infer that all sins involving the body affect it in the same way or to the same extent, we need to listen to these words from Paul:

> Flee from sexual immorality. Every other sin a person commits
> is outside the body, but the sexually immoral person sins against
> his own body. (1 Cor. 6:18)

The exact meaning of this verse is debated by scholars. But it's clear what it can't mean. Paul can't be saying that no sin apart from sexual sin is against the body in the sense of harming it. Many sins harm the body: alcoholism, substance abuse, gluttony, and suicide, to name just a few. All these do obvious harm to our body. Proper stewardship of our health involves far more (but not less) than abstaining from sexual sin. What Paul is saying is that there is a unique way in which sexual sin affects the body. It is not alone in having an impact on the body; it *is* unique in the way it does so. The clue as to what this means comes a few verses earlier:

> Do you not know that your bodies are members of Christ? Shall I then take the members of Christ and make them members of a prostitute? Never! Or do you not know that he who is joined to a prostitute becomes one body with her? For, as it is written, "The two will become one flesh." (1 Cor. 6:15–16)

There were Christians in Corinth visiting prostitutes. Perhaps they thought the body was so unspiritual that nothing consequential could really happen if they just indulged a few physical appetites. Their thinking seems to have been that God was interested in the spiritual rather than the physical. If their bodies had no spiritual significance, presumably it didn't really matter what they did with them. For some, that justified regular visits to the brothel.

Paul shows how catastrophically wrong this way of thinking is. Christians, he reminds them, are united to Christ. And that union involves every aspect of who we are, bodies included. So our "bodies are members of Christ" now. They are not irrelevant. Quite the opposite.

But more than that, Paul needs to remind them also of the other union being formed at the same time here, deeply incompatible with their union with Christ. Whether they intend it or not, by sleeping with a prostitute, they are uniting themselves to her as well. Paul says they become "one body with her." The "two becoming one flesh" idea is first introduced in the Bible in Genesis 2 following the union of Adam and Eve. But it is true not only of the sexual union that takes place within the covenant of marriage. This one-fleshing happens when a man has sex with his wife; it also happens when a man has sex with a prostitute. A "one body" union is still the result. Gordon Fee explains:

> To have sexual intercourse with a prostitute involves an illicit sexual joining of one's body to that of another (literally). It is not the sexual union itself that is incompatible with union with Christ; it is such a union *with a prostitute*.[2]

Sexual sin is unlike other sins in that it unites the body, whole-sale, to someone else. It involves the forming of a "one body" union, whether or not we intend it. It does something to and with the body that is not the case with other sins. Brian Rosner and Roy Ciampa conclude, "No other sin threatens to put the body under the mastery of something or someone else" in the way that sexual sin does.[3]

It is not that our body is untainted by sin, and then we sin sexually and now our body is brought into it. As we've seen, our body is implicated in our sin in innumerable ways. Sexual sin further enmeshes it in ways other sins are not able to.

To return to language we used earlier, our bodies always become ground zero for our sinful nature. No wonder Paul can describe them as bodies of death (Rom. 7:24). Every part of them has been a vehicle and site for our sin.

Given this, it is not hard to see why we feel such shame when we think about our body. We associate parts of our body with particular wrongs we have done—wrongs perhaps we now can't believe we did; wrongs we dearly wish had never taken place. The same can be true of sins in which the body was not as directly involved.

In Shakespeare's *Macbeth*, Lady Macbeth is complicit in the murder of King Duncan. She didn't literally lay a finger on him herself—her husband does the gruesome dirty work; she facilitates—but she is nevertheless plagued by a guilt-ridden conscience. In one famous scene she is sleepwalking and rubbing her hands together as though obsessively washing the blood of Duncan from them, saying, "Out, damned spot! Out, I say!" and "Will these hands ne'er be clean?"

It is one of the most insightful scenes Shakespeare ever wrote, one that was certainly ahead of its time in terms of understanding human psychology. It describes what we now understand to be a common response to deep guilt—a desperate sense of wanting somehow to be able to wash it away.

But of course shame does not just stem from sins we have committed; it can come as a result of having been sinned against. This too can define how we see our own body and lead to a profound sense of shame.

I think of someone I know who was often beaten at a young age by his father. He was hit in the face—a particularly psychologically damaging part of the body to receive blows, given how our face is really the locus of who we are to the outside world. Being hit here is perhaps more personal than being hit anywhere else. That this all happened at such a young and formative age only made the impact greater. My friend grew up with a deep sense of self-loathing, particularly about the way he looked. The only way he could process what had happened was to put the blame squarely on himself. *He* must be why he was being beaten. Well into adulthood he has hated his looks, associating them with the shame of what happened. That physical self-resentment led to self-harm and a pattern of unhealthy sexual behavior—a desperate attempt to provide sexual pleasure to older men.

My friend is now a Christian, seeing himself as God sees him and accepting the redemption of Christ (rather than attempting to redeem himself by physically pleasuring others), but the sense of shame has not entirely gone and remains something he continues to battle.

The sin of others can affect us in a complex multiplicity of ways, leading to all sorts of issues with our perception of our body. It is sadly not uncommon for victims of abuse to feel as though they are to blame and to assume the problem lies in their body rather than with those doing the abuse.

Death

The greatest evidence of our bodily brokenness is simultaneously ubiquitous and forced out of our minds so that we tend not to notice its significance—our bodies die.

We often don't connect death to our spiritual brokenness because we tend to think that the death of our body is somehow natural. In the Western world, we also try to avoid thinking about death as much as we can. Death for us was never meant to be our physical destiny. Paul writes:

> Just as sin came into the world through one man, and death through sin, . . . so death spread to all men because all sinned. (Rom. 5:12)

Death came through sin, Paul says. It was not part of our original design.

The creation narrative in Genesis makes this clear. When God first opened up the bounty of his creation to Adam and Eve, he had one stipulation:

> The Lord God commanded the man, saying, "You may surely eat of every tree of the garden, but of the tree of the knowledge of good and evil you shall not eat, for in the day that you eat of it you shall surely die." (Gen. 2:16–17)

We tend to read this and immediately ask the raft of questions it raises: "What was the tree of the knowledge of good and evil?" "Why was eating of it so bad?" But we mustn't miss the sheer abundance of freedom and provision here. Every tree of the garden was open to them. Just one—*one!*—was not.

To eat of this tree was to disobey God, to rebel against his authority. To break any command was rebellious, but this tree was especially significant. It represented knowing good and evil the way God knows good and evil—not merely being aware of it, but being the one who is uniquely able to determine it. To eat from this tree was not only to break God's law but to take upon oneself the right to make God's law, the right that properly belongs to God alone. It was to assume man actually knows more than God does about how we should live and what should be regarded as good and bad. This was the sin God was warning against. The punishment of that sin with death was not arbitrary. To sin by eating from that tree was to push God out of his rightful place and substitute man instead. It was to turn away from the God who is life. That can only lead to death.

111

Yet when Eve and then Adam ate this fruit and committed this sin, they did not immediately die. When the devil tempted Eve, he had said to her, "You will not surely die" (Gen. 3:4). So perhaps in those first moments after disobeying this command, Adam and Eve thought the devil was right: *We did eat, and we didn't die.* The fact that death was not immediate was God's mercy. Even at this early point in the biblical narrative we see God's grace. He still had a plan for humanity. He preserved them. But though death was not immediate, it had become inevitable. So God said to them, "For you are dust, and to dust you shall return" (Gen. 3:19).

I am writing this on my laptop. I don't have the charger with me. At the moment my battery is at 58 percent. My threshold for starting to feel panicky is probably anything under 30 percent. So right now the game is to see how much I can write before the battery dies and I have to leave and find the charger. It could be another couple of hours. But one thing is certain: it will surely die. Once I unplugged the laptop from the charger and marched off without it, it was inevitable that it would die.

The same is true of us. Once we have, as it were, unplugged ourselves from the source of all life, death will inevitably result. This is what Paul means when he says, "Death spread to all men because all sinned" (Rom. 5:12). The proof that we share in this sin is that we share in its consequences. Death comes to us all:

> It is appointed for man to die once, and after that comes judgment. (Heb. 9:27)

Our "deathday" is just as fixed as our birthday. We just don't know when it is.

It has been well observed that we are not nearly as aware of death as earlier generations. This is partly the result of a good thing. Matthew McCullough writes:

> The remarkable achievements of modern medicine have pushed death further and further back in the average Western person's life span. We enjoy better disease prevention, better pharmaceutical treatments, and better emergency care than any other society in history.[4]

McCullough continues:

> At the end of the eighteenth century, four out of five people died before the age of seventy. Average life expectancy was in the late thirties. Now the *average* is nearly eighty years old.[5]

We rejoice at these advances. I think of some of the health issues I've had or that people very close to me have had, and it is sobering to think that even a few decades ago, these could easily have been fatal in a way they are not today.

But much of our lack of awareness of death is not due to medical change but to cultural change. The reality is that we in the West *really* don't like thinking about death. It's a downer. If it doesn't need to be thought about now, why put ourselves through the misery?

In the 2000 Leonardo DiCaprio movie *The Beach*, a group of travelers has formed a secret community on an inaccessible and picturesque island off the coast of Thailand. They have their own paradise and are determined to enjoy it at any cost. When a shark attacks their fishing party, one dies and another, Christo, is seriously injured. They can't take him to the hospital as that will risk exposing their community, so Christo is forced to remain, moaning in agony. It begins to affect morale. The lead character Richard explains:

> After the funeral we all tried to get back to normal, but it just didn't seem right. Pretty soon it became clear that the problem was Christo. You see, in a shark attack, or any other major tragedy I guess, the important thing is to get eaten and die, in which case there's a funeral and somebody makes a speech and everybody says what a good guy you were, or get better in which case everyone can forget about it.[6]

But Christo hadn't died and he hadn't recovered. He just lay there in agony, very slowly dying. So they removed him from the camp so that they could be spared the gruesome reality of seeing him suffer and die. Richard concludes, "Out of sight really was out of mind. Once he was gone we felt a whole lot better."[7] The film pretty much sums up our attitude to dying and death: keep it out of sight. Don't let it spoil the enjoyment of life.

The first church I ever belonged to was a seven-hundred-year-old Church of England congregation. The pathway from the parking lot to the church door took us through a churchyard, a common feature of these historical churches by design. What could better remind you that you were part of the fellowship of the living and the dead? You would literally pass the saints in glory on your way to gather as saints on earth.

Death was more visible in everyday life in previous generations. We have pushed it to the margins. Matthew McCullough again:

> Now the expectation of death has shifted from a familiar event in a familiar place—an event that occurred at the centre of

life—to sanitized, professionalized institutions that most people rarely visit.[8]

But airbrushing out the reality of death does nothing to diminish its certainty. It just leaves us in a state of near-constant denial. We make every effort to physically distance ourselves from death. But it doesn't change the reality that we have to face it. Uncomfortable though we are with the fact, we will die. It isn't hypothetical. It isn't something that happens only to other people. One day, perhaps sooner than we ever imagined, we will have to face it ourselves. Determination to avoid thinking about it is just escapism.

There is a moment in C. S. Lewis's novel *That Hideous Strength* when the main character, Mark, is confronted by the reality of his own death:

> He had never till now been at close quarters with death. Now, glancing down at his hand (because his hands were cold and he had been automatically rubbing them), it came to him as a totally new idea that this very hand, with its five nails and the yellow tobacco-stain on the inside of the second finger, would one day be the hand of a corpse, and later the hand of a skeleton.[9]

It is an arresting thought. Look at your hand now. One day it will be lifeless. The nails will turn purple. The skin will decompose. The color, the freckles and hairs, the bright vein running along the back. Eventually all that will be left is the bones. To dust we shall return. As Bill Bryson writes:

> There are thousands of things that can kill us—slightly more than eight thousand, according to the *International Statistical*

Classification of Diseases and Related Health Problems compiled by the World Health Organisation—and we escape every one of them but one.[10]

It is inevitable. "No one can avoid death," writes Timothy Keller. "It has been said that all the wars and plagues have never raised the death toll—it has always been one for each and every person."[11]

But awareness of death in the Bible is not meant to be something that interferes with the real stuff of life; it is meant to bring clarity and focus to it. Nowhere is this clearer perhaps than Psalm 90, written by Moses. He begins by reflecting on God as eternal:

> Before the mountains were brought forth,
>> or ever you had formed the earth and the world,
>> from everlasting to everlasting you are God. (Ps. 90:2)

To whichever horizon Moses looked—eternity past or eternity future—God was there. There was a point in time before the mountains existed or the earth came to be, when God was still there. Always and forever. Our own mortality is brought into sharp focus in contrast:

> The years of our life are seventy,
>> or even by reason of strength eighty. (Ps. 90:10)

Even eighty—truly a ripe old age in the ancient world—is unavoidably finite. The apostle James puts it even more starkly:

> What is your life? For you are a mist that appears for a little time and then vanishes. (James 4:14)

116

In my bathroom every morning the steam from the shower mists up the mirror. To be able to look in the mirror after I've showered, all I need to do is open the window. In just a matter of moments the mist has disappeared. I can watch it happening. This is what our lives are like.

Our perception when we are young is that the years stretching out ahead of us are virtually infinite. But there is a reason everyone feels life to be short. It is. When we look over the fence at eternity, we become even more aware that our own time slot here is unimpressively short. My grandfather is one hundred and two years old. When he was born, the First World War was still in full swing. And yet all he can say is how quickly it has all gone. Yet this is meant to be the point. Moses is not having a downer when he reflects on these things in Psalm 90. He is having a moment of realization:

So teach us to number our days
  that we may get a heart of wisdom. (Ps. 90:12)

Numbering our days is another way of saying that we have a healthy awareness of our own finiteness. Our time is limited. Knowing that clarifies what life needs to be about. Numbering our days protects us from delusion and escapism. It is key to getting "a heart of wisdom." We will not think rightly about life on earth and what matters most if we live in willful oblivion to our death. If God alone is eternal, then it is only by having life with him that we can live in a way that won't be mocked by our inevitable death. Our seventy years (or eighty, or one hundred and two) will not feel too short if it turns out they are not the only life we will have, and certainly not if they are not the best life we will have. Only by being pulled into the life of God himself can death become anything other than a grim full stop at the end of our lives.

Until then, though, death is the most potent reminder that our bodies are broken. Even as we live, even if we are in relatively good health, the specter of death in our own body is unavoidable. Not only is the aging process itself a testimony to the decline our body will inevitably face, but our very skin cells are continually turning to dust all around us:

> We shed skin cells copiously, almost carelessly; some twenty-five thousand flakes a minute, over a million pieces every hour. Run a finger along a dusty shelf and you are in large part clearing a path through fragments of your former self. Silently and remorselessly we turn to dust.[12]

To dust we indeed return. Even while we are living.

Death is the climax and ultimate proof of our bodily brokenness. But it is not the end of the story. We've thought about some of the principal ways we encounter this brokenness—affliction and shame, sin and death—but our own experience of brokenness, extreme though it may be for some, is not itself the ultimate experience of brokenness humanity has ever faced. There was one body more broken than any of ours, and it is through that ultimate brokenness that we find the answer to our own.

A Body You Have Prepared for Me

The Broken Body of Jesus

I CAN STILL REMEMBER the first DVD I ever owned: 1999's *The Matrix*. Not only was it wonderful to see all the groundbreaking effects and stunts in amazing new clarity; I also got to enjoy the whole new concept of bonus features. These became a huge selling point.

Bonus features are great for nerdy types like me. In those included on *The Matrix* DVD, the directors talked through various creative choices. *So that's why it looked so cool.* The set-piece effects wizardry was all explained. *So that's how they did that.* Basically all the behind-the-scenes beans were spilled.

Some people hate all this, of course. They'd rather just see the movie and leave the magic unexplained. But it gives me more appreciation for the movie rather than less. Even a bad movie is somewhat improved by hearing those behind it talk through what they were at least trying to accomplish.

The Bible gives us unique insight into the brokenness of creation, including our bodies. Paul has shown us that the world has been subjected to futility by God himself such that it does not work properly. What bewilders us in nature is explained to us in Scripture. So we, of all people, should understand and appreciate the extent to which this world is fallen. God has given us a unique backstage pass into why this has happened and what it means. We should be able to make sense of it in a way that no one else can. It's like we've been given exclusive access to all the best DVD extra features: explaining what is really going on, showing us behind the scenes, and above all giving us the words of the Creator himself to help us understand why things are the way they are.

This insight should, at the very least, make us unusually compassionate. When we see people going through the throes of bodily brokenness—perhaps some chronic illness, or the recurrent pain of body shame, or having to pick their way through the wreckage of some sexual sin—we have no reason to stand aloof, as if these things are beneath us or somehow make those people less worthy than us. When someone is going through something we've never had to face personally, it is all too easy to adopt a mindset of "pull yourself together" even if we would never actually say those words. Yes, where sin has taken place, there is personal responsibility and culpability, but this does not justify a cold attitude or a lack of sympathy as the sinner wrestles with the aftermath.

It was a few years ago that I first met someone who experiences gender dysphoria. A mutual friend introduced us, and this individual—I'll call him Max—was kind enough to spend an afternoon talking me through his story. I've struggled with all sorts of sins and temptations, but I've never experienced gender dysphoria. I've never not felt male or desired to be female. There are plenty of other ways my desires and wants have been twisted by sin, but this has not been one of them.

There were two ways I felt I needed to relate to this new friend. The first was to make clear that I had never gone through what he was experiencing. I couldn't come close to saying, "I know just how you feel." I didn't. Max was articulate and honest enough to help me understand what he was dealing with far more than I'd been able to beforehand. But there was no obvious and neat correspondence between his trial and any I had faced. His experience was quite different from mine.

At the same time, though I couldn't claim to know his experience, I could show him that we are all in this together. Romans 8 puts us in the same boat—we're all making our way as fallen people through life in a fallen creation. However alien his experience might seem to me, we are definitely part of the same tragically broken species. At that more fundamental level I could identify with him.

None of this is to say there is no place for moral evaluation. There were certainly some urgent biblical truths my friend and I needed to discuss. There were, to my mind, a number of significantly unbiblical ways he was thinking about his situation which, if pursued, would only take him further from God's will for him. We had some hard and raw discussions. But at the same time, my understanding of our shared fallen humanity meant that there was no reason for me to feel superior or look down on him or to be in any way judgmental. It is not as if I'm gliding through life unscathed by the fall.

It should be this perspective that enables us as Christians to be people of grace and truth whatever situation we find ourselves in or responding to. If the occurrences of brokenness we are most conscious of are our own and not those of others, we will be heading in the right direction. However unlike our own experience others' experiences are, we won't dismiss them or push them away. We're all made of the same stuff and subjected to the same frustration. Christians should be the most compassionate people on the planet.

The Sympathy of Christ

Of course, we will never be more than a pale reflection of Christ himself. However much we can understand and sympathize with the plight of others, there will always be limits—aspects of their experience we can't identify with, ways it plays out in their life quite differently from ours. But with Christ, there is never a lack of understanding. However much we "get it," he gets it more. Not because he is more fallen (quite the opposite!), but because no one has ever experienced the full ravages of this fallen world more than Jesus. There is no form of human suffering he doesn't understand better than we do. This is how the writer of the letter to the Hebrews puts it:

> For we do not have a high priest who is unable to sympathize with our weaknesses, but one who in every respect has been tempted as we are, yet without sin. Let us then with confidence draw near to the throne of grace, that we may receive mercy and find grace to help in time of need. (Heb. 4:15–16)

We've all had the experience of someone being unsympathetic toward us. We come with pain or need and are met with a blank stare or a sigh of frustration. We're treated like a problem or a nuisance at the very moment we actually need tenderness and understanding. It can easily leave us worse off: our original problem is compounded by this additional insensitivity.

At other times there might be people who genuinely *want* to understand but are just unable to. They see that someone is troubled. They long to enter into what is going on and to see why it has been so hard, but they can't. The type of pain is so far outside their own field of experience. Hebrews 4:15–16 shows us that Jesus is not like that. He is not "unable to sympathize." He isn't bemused when we turn to him in our pain. He gets it. In fact, he understands it all more than even we do. We're told why. He is one "who in every respect has been tempted as we are, yet without sin."

In order to be the perfect high priest for us—to be the one who can perfectly mediate between us and God—Jesus has to be *like us* in just the right way and *unlike us* in just the right way. The passage shows us how. Jesus has been "tempted as we are." When he lived on this earth, he was not sheltered from its hardships. It is jokingly said of the Queen of England that everywhere she goes, all she can smell is fresh paint. But Jesus's experience of human life was unvarnished, unsanitized. His life was not one Instagrammable moment after another.

But there's more. Jesus was not only tempted "as we are" but "in every respect." His hardship was not of one narrow kind, such that he could relate to those of us who had also experienced it but to no one else. His experience of this world's fallenness was comprehensive. He ran the full gauntlet. This is not to say that Jesus must have experienced every single temptation we can think up. We are not saying he had to have been tempted by, say, lesbianism, or wasting too much time on video games. We're saying that there is no species of trial he is unfamiliar with. Dane Ortlund sums it up:

> He knows what it is to be thirsty, hungry, despised, rejected, scorned, shamed, embarrassed, abandoned, misunderstood,

falsely accused, suffocated, tortured, and killed. He knows what it is to be lonely.[1]

There is no human agony unfamiliar to Jesus. With each and every kind, he is able to sympathize. He would be a deficient high priest if he could not.

But he is also unlike us in the way we need him to be. The verse in Hebrews says he "has been tempted as we are, *yet without sin.*" This is where Jesus is crucially different from us. We are so quickly ensnared in temptation because our hearts are sinful. Before we're even barely aware of what's going on, we can already be in way over our head. Sin has a natural ally deep within us. It really doesn't take much to get us running toward it.

But Jesus is without sin. He experienced temptation in the wilderness, but in a key respect his temptations were quite unlike ours. He is like us in that he experienced them, but quite unlike us in that such temptations were utterly alien to his heart. He had no internal landing pad for them in the way that we do. So, internally in his heart and attitude and externally in all he did, he was without sin. Dane Ortlund again sums up why this is so significant: "He himself is not trapped in the hole of sin with us; he alone can pull us out."[2]

If he was able to sympathize with us, but only because he was in the exact same predicament, his sympathy would be genuine but of no benefit to us. If he was mired in his own sin, he would not be able to help us in ours. Or if in his sinlessness he was utterly aloof, as though every human trial and foible were utterly beyond him, his sinlessness would leave him quite remote and unsympathetic. He could not be a high priest who represented us, because he would not be able to identify and stand with us in the ways that we need him to. But as a truly tested but sinless man, Jesus is able to sympathize and help. He understands. He knows more about the brokenness of this world than we ever will. So there is no area of bodily brokenness and human suffering he doesn't know far more about than we do.

Physical Pain

We know it well, in different ways and to varying extents. We each have our own stories and our own medicine cabinets. But Jesus's experience of physical suffering was not shallow. He experienced bodily pain at its furthest extreme.

We don't know if, during the course of his life, Jesus ever faced a particular sickness or had allergies or suffered a physical injury. We are told nothing of his medical history. The Gospel writers were unconcerned with that detail. But each Gospel shows something of the extraordinary physical suffering he experienced at the end of his life. We may think immediately of the cross when we consider his physical suffering. But while this was clearly the most brutal part of his experience, it was not where his hardship began. He had already endured enormous brutality up to this point.

Jesus's predictions of his death included all of it. He said that "the Son of Man must suffer many things" (Mark 8:31); that "they will mock him and spit on him, and flog him and kill him" (Mark 10:34). We see this reflected in the accounts. When in the custody of the Jewish authorities, Jesus was beaten both before and during his time before the ruling assembly (Matt. 26:67–68; Luke 22:63–62). But it was at the hands of the Romans that Jesus received his most severe beating.

Again, the details are sparse. Matthew simply says that Pilate "released for them Barabbas, and having scourged Jesus, delivered him to be crucified" (Matt. 27:26). *Scourged* is a word we are typically unfamiliar with. It describes a well-established and documented

Roman practice of severely beating a prisoner, normally with a multi-lashed whip that had embedded fragments of bone and metal so as to maximize the amount of flesh torn. The aim was to reduce someone's flesh to a bloody pulp. It is quite unimaginable to most of us today.

We're then told of the crown of thorns thrust onto Jesus's head, which, along with the scarlet robe, was meant to be a parody of the claim that he was King. We don't tend to stop and think about this aspect of his suffering, but such a crown was very bloody and painful. Those of us familiar with the wider biblical narrative note that thorns were part of God's judgment on the earth in response to Adam and Eve's sin, so Jesus is literally being crowned with our curse.

All that demonstrates that Jesus was no stranger to the extremes of physical suffering. When we find ourselves facing severe pain, whether through illness, injury, or the brutality of others, we can be assured that Jesus is not unsympathetic. He understands our pain and turmoil. He gets it. We can turn to him. As the writer to the Hebrews earlier encouraged us, "Let us then with confidence draw near to the throne of grace, that we may receive mercy and find grace to help in time of need" (Heb. 4:16). As we come to this Jesus, we can be assured he is not only not lacking in sympathy but is also brimful of mercy and grace.

The fact is, no one was more familiar with bodily pain than Jesus. His sorrows were more than physical, of course—he knew intense emotional and spiritual turmoil too. But as we face our own physical trials, there is one who will always hear us with full compassion and understanding.

Whatever our physical affliction or infirmity, the bodily sufferings of Christ are how we know that one day we will find ourselves in a new creation where there will be no more tears. Jesus did not endure all that he did merely to be in a position to understand us fully, but also—through his own suffering—to secure for us a bodily existence in the age to come where there will be no brokenness at all. He was broken so that we might one day be healed. Our pain now, however intense, is not ultimate.

Shame

The various forms of shame we feel because of our body are also not unknown to Jesus. We're not told much about his physical appearance, beyond what would be typical for a man born in that part of the world around that time. We don't have details about his height or weight or build. But we do know that he would have been, to his own people, quite ordinary in his looks:

> He had no form or majesty that we should look at him,
> and no beauty that we should desire him. (Isa. 53:2)

Much about beauty is subjective, but there are still people, even in real life, who are unusually good-looking, men and women others tend to notice. According to that prophecy from Isaiah, Jesus was not such a person. There was nothing about his looks to draw attention. Whatever drew people to him, it wasn't appearance or outward beauty. Jesus was (obviously) utterly exceptional in a • whole host of ways, but his looks were not part of that. So if we find ourselves to be quite unremarkable in appearance, we are in good company.

But Isaiah's prophecy goes further. In life Jesus is, visually, nothing special to look at. But in his suffering, he is actually something to look away from:

As many were astonished at you—
  his appearance was so marred, beyond human semblance,
  and his form beyond that of the children of mankind. . . .
He was despised and rejected by men,
  a man of sorrows and acquainted with grief;
as one from whom men hide their faces
  he was despised, and we esteemed him not. (Isa. 52:14; 53:3)

We are used to the idea of "rubberneckers," people who slow down on the road just to be able to get a good look at a wreck on the other side. Maybe we've done that ourselves. We sometimes have an odd fascination with these things, a weird sense of wanting to be in the moment and know what has happened. We've all been stuck in traffic that turned out to be caused by nothing more than a steady succession of motorists doing just this. But there is a point where fascination turns to revulsion, where something is so hideous that we can't bear to see it.

Isaiah's prophecy points to how Christ would be so afflicted by others that he would barely look human anymore. This time, people would be twisting their necks not to look at the spectacle, but to look away from it.

Some of us feel that we are hideous to look at. Something in our experience has taught us to assume that and to feel a deep sense of shame when someone else sets eyes on us. We don't want to be noticed or seen. A friend of mine felt this way for some time. She would only let us take her out if she got into the back of the car behind us without us seeing her. At other times she was able to cope with certain friends facing her. For many others of us, it is nothing as extreme as that, but we still feel a sense of deep shame about some aspect of how we look. Someone told me once that he felt that the way he looked made him feel like a walking target, and that it was just a matter of time before people would notice and dislike him.

There is so much to say to this, of course. But it is surely significant for someone who feels this way to realize that Jesus does know what it is like to experience utter shame. What was done to him in his final hours was so severe that it caused people to physically turn away, to avoid setting eyes on him. For some of us, our shame, when it comes to our bodies, may be more perceived than real. But Jesus's shame was ultimate. However we might be feeling, he knows what it is really and truly like, more than anyone else.

Paradoxically, it is only by looking to the one who bore ultimate shame that we can find a way forward with our own:

> I sought the LORD, and he answered me
> and delivered me from all my fears.
> Those who look to him are radiant,
> and their faces shall never be ashamed. (Ps. 34:4–5)

The one who plumbed the depths of ultimate shame is the one who can lift us up into the place of never having to face it. He is the one who answers when we call on him, who delivers when we are helpless before all that could overwhelm us. And the result is our "faces shall never be ashamed." He will never let us down. He had to become shame so that we could find a way out of it. He had to be engulfed in it so that we could be shielded from it.

So "those who look to him are radiant." This is worthy of consideration. It's clearly not saying that those who look to Jesus have their looks improved. But it is saying that looking to him will do something in us that causes us to be radiant.

Many of us have encountered people who are outwardly attractive but inwardly very unattractive. As we see that inner unattractiveness, it colors how we see their looks. Looks matter very little if they are not matched by character: "Like a gold ring in a pig's snout is a beautiful woman without discretion" (Prov. 11:22). The beauty of the gold ring is entirely offset by the pig it is attached to. Physical attractiveness is just as easily offset by a lack of character. Looks are very superficial.

Looks are also short-lived. "Charm is deceptive, and beauty is fleeting" (Prov. 31:30 NIV). Our relative attractiveness can change significantly over time. We age, we have accidents, we get sick, or our hard living takes its toll on how we look. But there is such a thing as an inner beauty that is unfading (1 Pet. 3:4), which is what we see reflected in Psalm 34. It's a real beauty that does not diminish with the aging process or the vagaries of life in this world. And it is not about what we look *like*, but what we look *at*; not *how* we look, but *where* we look: "Those who look to him are radiant."

I mentioned my friend Shelby, who had been made to feel less of a man due to his height. He recently wrote to me:

> I found that I had grown so much in the Lord over the last 10 years that it didn't bother me as much. I think it comes only with the security of knowing in my head and heart that God does not make mistakes and I am the way I am for a specific God-ordained purpose . . . that it would be wrong if I were any other way than the way I am. In God's sovereignty, I am not tall, dark, and handsome—I'm short, white, and funny. Coveting a taller me for all those years was foolishness because I was wanting a not-God-designed me.

Body Dysphoria

One particularly acute form of bodily brokenness that we have touched upon is gender dysphoria, the experience of feeling that you do not match your physiological gender. As Christians we need to take issue with much of the thinking around this discussion and how the givenness of our bodies is set aside so that inner feelings are given priority. As I have attempted to demonstrate, the Bible shows us that maleness and femaleness are both biologically grounded rather than psychologically determined. But while much of the thinking may be deficient, the pain experienced is very real. Tim and Kathy Keller observe:

> To have your feelings sharply out of accord with your body is a life-dominating grief. As Christians, we of all people should be able to show understanding and compassion, knowing how the fall (Genesis 3) has twisted what God pronounced "good" when he made humanity into a binary-gendered reflection of his nature.[3]

We all experience the curse of the fall in bodily ways. But the answer to the problems in our body—along with the answer to any of our problems—is never going to be found in our body itself. Nothing we can do to our body will help us to feel that we're our true self—at least not in a true and lasting way. We can alter our appearance; we can change much of what we think to be wrong. But we will never find the real freedom we so deeply crave.

No, we need to look again to the ultimate brokenness of Christ's body. As we've seen, he experienced the ultimate affliction. His was the body most reviled by others. He never experienced gender dysphoria, but when he "who had no sin" was "made . . . sin for us" (2 Cor. 5:21 NIV), it was the ultimate experience of being in the wrong flesh. There was no greater dysphoria ever experienced. And he went through all of that for us. As Tim and Kathy Keller remind us:

> Only through being in Christ's body—through the change in identity that comes from being a child in his family—does anyone find ultimate relief from their sense of dislocation in the world.[4]

Real bodily hope is found only in Christ.

Death

The ultimate sign and experience of bodily brokenness, as we've seen, is death itself. With good reason Paul calls it "the last enemy" (1 Cor. 15:26).

Once again, the Gospel accounts describe his actual death in little detail. "He breathed his last" (Luke 23:46). But there is no doubting the historical accuracy of what happened. Jesus not only died, but his death was further confirmed by a soldier piercing his side to make sure, and his burial was witnessed by some of his followers. Jesus didn't have a near-death experience or a metaphorical death. He actually, truly died.

And yet he was the one human being who didn't deserve to die. We have already considered how death is the inevitable consequence of sin—Paul refers to it as "the wages of sin" (Rom. 6:23). But Jesus committed no sin. He is the only person whose death makes no natural sense. But of course Jesus had told us that his death was not on account of any sin of his own:

> For even the Son of Man came not to be served but to serve, and to give his life as a ransom for many. (Mark 10:45)

His death was for others—"for many." It was not the outworking
of sin in his life but a ransom for us on account of the sin in our lives.
This is why he was so determined to die. He insisted that "the Son
of Man must . . . be killed" (Mark 8:31). *Must* be killed. Not *might*.
It wasn't just a possibility; it was his destiny to die. When it came,
he wanted his disciples to understand that his death was not a sign
that everything had gone wrong but that everything had gone right.

So it is by his death that our death can be defeated. We still face
our earthly death, but it no longer has the same devastating meaning.

> When the perishable puts on the imperishable, and the mortal
> puts on immortality, then shall come to pass the saying that is
> written:
>
> > "Death is swallowed up in victory."
> > "O death, where is your victory?
> >   O death, where is your sting?" (1 Cor. 15:54–55)

Death is no longer the sign of judgment and defeat, but the
entryway into new life with Christ. As we shall see, we will not
be done with bodily life. We shall enjoy physical life in the new
creation—life with no specter of death hanging over it. "Your death
is not an end but a beginning. Not a wall, but a door. Not an exit,
but an entrance."[5] All this comes through Jesus yielding his own
body up to death:

> He himself bore our sins in *his body* on the tree. (1 Pet. 2:24)

> And by that will we have been sanctified through the offering of
> *the body of Jesus* Christ once for all. (Heb. 10:10)

But now he has reconciled you by *Christ's physical body* through death. (Col. 1:22 NIV)

The problems we experience *with* our body were never ultimately going to be solved *by* our body. We may be able to ameliorate some aspects of our bodily brokenness—we can cure some ills and ease some pains. But we cannot fix what has been broken. The only hope for us is the body of Jesus, broken fully and finally for us. And by looking to his broken body we find true hope for our own.

In Christ, our bodies are no longer identified by what we do *with* them, or by what others have done *to* them, but by what Jesus has done *for* them. And so we await "the redemption of our bodies" (Rom. 8:23) with patience. And in the meantime, we learn what it means to use our bodies for our new master and Savior.

PART 3

———————

REDEEMED BODIES

8

A Temple of the Holy Spirit

The Body and Christ

IT IS HARD TO IMAGINE anything more horrific than being owned by someone else—to find yourself belonging wholly to another. For some, tragically, it does not require imagination.

A dear friend of mine was sold into sex slavery as a young woman. It was a period that left many physical and nonphysical scars. It taught her to detach herself from her body. It was no longer hers. "My body never belonged to me anyway—everyone always took it," she told me recently. She was eventually able to escape and start a new life. During the course of it all, she became a Christian. These words from the Bible have come to be precious to her:

You are not your own, for you were bought with a price. (1 Cor. 6:19–20)

They had been true in an awful, dehumanizing sense. They were now true in a life-giving and supremely dignifying sense.

The idea of someone being bought sounds justifiably awful to our ears. Human fallenness is such that we cannot be trusted with the responsibility of owning another human being. We make terrible masters of one another. It is why human trafficking is prohibited in the Bible as something unspeakably evil.

We've been thinking about how broken our bodies are and about how wonderfully Jesus stepped into ultimate bodily brokenness so that we could be restored again. But Jesus does not merely tinker with us from afar, fixing us up while keeping his distance. He has brought us to himself, and we could not be closer. He has united us to himself. Another dimension of this union is that we now belong to him. We are his, fully. But he hasn't bullied his way into power over us. He hasn't coerced or manipulated us. And he hasn't stolen us. He has bought us with a price—the price of his own precious life laid down for us.

The only way our bodies can be restored and redeemed by Jesus is through them *belonging* to Jesus.

The Christians in Corinth had a skewed view of the body. Various slogans were doing the rounds in the church community there, slogans that summed up the prevailing way of thinking, like hashtags for us today. Here's one of them:

All things are lawful for me. (1 Cor. 6:12)

In other words, as a Christian I'm free. I'm not bound by some external set of rules. Christ has given me freedom, so I can do what I want.

There is an element of truth in this. We *do* have freedom as Christians. Our standing before God is not based on compliance to laws and rules. The law given by God in the Old Testament was never intended to give us the impression that we have the capacity to obey our way into God's favor. Actually, the law was given for the opposite reason, to show us that we don't have what it takes to be the people we are meant to be, and that we will be able to relate to God only on the basis of his forgiveness.

So, yes, in this sense, we are free from law. Our status before God is not grounded in such things. Just a couple of pages later, Paul himself goes on to ask, "Am I not free?" (1 Cor. 9:1). The implied positive answer is so obvious that he doesn't need to supply it.

But our freedom in Christ doesn't mean we are entirely without obligation of any kind. Paul is, as he puts it, "under the law of Christ" (1 Cor. 9:21). "He is not bound by the law of Moses but is bound to obey God as one living under the authority of Christ."[1] Our freedom in Christ in no way means we have no moral obligations.

Yet this was apparently what many of the Corinthian Christians believed. This slogan—"All things are lawful for me"—was being used to excuse behavior that was forbidden to Christians. So Paul responds initially with a couple of his own slogans:

"All things are lawful for me," but not all things are helpful. "All things are lawful for me," but I will not be dominated by anything. (1 Cor. 6:12)

They may feel free to be doing what they're doing. But what they're doing is, first, not helpful and, second, actually harmful.

God's ways for his people to live are not arbitrary. God hasn't drawn the behavioral lines that he's drawn for us simply because they had to be drawn *somewhere*, and they could just as easily have been drawn somewhere else. My extended family has an annual boules tournament. Each year no one can remember how many points you're officially meant to have to win, so we set our own. It varies from year to year, depending on what we feel like. Seven points one year; five another. But God's ways for us are not like that. When he gives us commandments, it is for our good. He made us and knows what is best for us. When we go outside his will for us, it is, as Paul is at pains to point out here, not going to help us. In fact, it could enslave us. Sin is not just wrong in some abstract sense. It is wrong in that it contradicts how God has meant us to live. Not every sin is directly and immediately harmful in a way that is obvious to all. Many sins are more subtle. But they can set us on a course that we might never have intended to go, and now we're doing things we never imagined doing and find ourselves feeling powerless to stop doing. As Jesus said, "Everyone who practices sin is a slave to sin" (John 8:34).

The real issue was how the Corinthians viewed the body and how this led them to particularly justify sexual sin. Paul quotes another of their slogans:

Food is meant for the stomach and the stomach for food.
(1 Cor. 6:13)

We can see where this is going. We have a bodily appetite for food. So when we get hungry, we eat. Stomachs need food; food is meant to be eaten. The same logic was being used to justify sexual sin. This too is another physical appetite that is meant to be satisfied when we find ourselves hungry for it. Both these are just a matter of biology. Food is about the intake of calories; sex is about the exchange of bodily fluids. The Corinthians thought neither to have lasting spiritual or moral significance.

But all of this rests on a key and mistaken assumption about the body. New Testament scholars Roy Ciampa and Brian Rosner summarize as follows:

> In a style typical of Greek dualistic thought, the Corinthians apparently reasoned that God is concerned only with those aspects of a person that survive death, that is, their soul or spirit.[2]

This is how so many still tend to think. God is only interested with the "spiritual" side of us. Our body is not relevant to his purposes, other than being the present and impermanent receptacle of our soul. Our eternal state (so it is believed) will be spiritual and not physical. So our physicality now is a temporary expedient rather than something of lasting value.

We can see this thinking impacting the Corinthians in a couple of ways at the same time. For some of them, this low view of the body meant they could do what they wanted with the body without thinking it would have any bearing on their relationship with God. So they dove into sexual sin. For others, the same low view of the body meant they thought bodily things were unspiritual and beneath them, so they were abstaining even from good things like sex within marriage, or from marriage altogether. Both licentiousness and asceticism came from this common belief about the body.

So Paul hits back with another hashtag that gets right to the heart of it all:

> The body is not meant for sexual immorality, but for the Lord, and the Lord for the body. (1 Cor. 6:13)

This single statement pulls the rug out from under them.

The Body Is for the Lord

Our body is not our own personal playground. It is not for *us*, in this sense. It is for the Lord. It is meant to be oriented toward him, to be used for him. It is not spiritually irrelevant. It has a purpose that is found in service to God. He has a plan for our whole self, body included.

The Lord Is for the Body

God is not indifferent to our body. He himself is spirit, but that does not mean he has no interest in our physicality. He is the one who made us physical, after all. He is not against our body, but for it, affirming it in creation and in Christ's coming in bodily form, and affirming it in his future plans to fully redeem it. Our body may be fallen, but that does not mean that God regrets making it or has changed his position on it. He is still pro-matter. The proof of all this is what Paul says next:

> God raised the Lord and will also raise us up by his power.
> (1 Cor. 6:14)

Jesus's body was not a temporary necessity. It is hard to think of a bigger affirmation of human bodies than the incarnation and resurrection of Jesus. Not only did he become fully and physically human, but Jesus has remained so. And the resurrection of Jesus points to the resurrection we will all one day experience as his people. Paul will outline the connection between the two later in his letter, and we will consider it later in this book.

The main point for us to see here is that if our bodies will one day be raised, then they have a future. And if they have a future, they are not insignificant now. Paul has removed the foundation the Corinthians had based their (un)ethical behavior on. The body really does matter. God's eternal plan for us involves our body. We can't write off our physical life as spiritually irrelevant.

The significance of our body in the future is a reflection of its significance in the present. This is what Paul turns to next. As he does so, he three times says to his readers, "Do you not know . . . ?"

Do you not know that your bodies are members of Christ? (6:15)

Or do you not know that he who is joined to a prostitute becomes one body with her? (6:16)

Or do you not know that your body is a temple of the Holy Spirit . . . ? (6:19)

In each case, Paul is showing how our body is not entirely self-contained. It is connected to and bound up with key external realities. It is a member of Christ—part of his body—and a temple of his Spirit. And when we sleep with someone, our body becomes one with that person.

These truths were not unfamiliar to the Corinthians. They should have known these things because they'd been taught them before. Their actions were simply showing how little they had understood key truths about their bodies. Their problem wasn't ignorance.

There are times when we don't need to be taught something new but reminded of something old. The renowned writer and lexicographer Samuel Johnson once said, "People need to be reminded more often than they need to be instructed." The issue isn't what we don't know, but remembering and acting on what we do know.

This was the case for the Corinthians when it came to beliefs about the body. Despite what they had been taught, they had collectively slid into a way of thinking that marginalized the place of the body in their Christianity. We must assume we are no less prone to doing the same thing. So as Paul tells them again of these foundational and staggering truths about their bodies, we need to pay careful attention.

Your Body Belongs to Jesus

Paul reminds them that their bodies are "members of Christ." Each individual believer's body now fully belongs to Jesus. We tend to think of being members of something as a somewhat voluntary arrangement. I'm a member of a gym, or a choir, or a company's loyalty program. Being a member typically means nothing more than that I'm choosing to stick around because I want the perks of membership but have the full freedom to disassociate the moment I believe it's not worth it. So hearing that we are "members of Christ" might give us the misleading impression that we've signed up to a spiritual scheme that doesn't have any kind of binding obligation.

This could not be further from the truth. Being members of Christ means we are inextricably bound up with him. Being a believer is not a matter of having once given Jesus our vote of confidence, or admiring him from afar, or even just trusting him in a vague sense now. Being a believer unites us to Jesus spiritually. All that we are is now joined to all that he is. Everything that flows to us from him flows to us through this union. But it also completely defines who we now are and how we live, including how we think about and use our bodies. So Paul applies this directly and bluntly to the Corinthian Christians who have been visiting prostitutes:

> Shall I then take the members of Christ and make them members of a prostitute? Never! (1 Cor. 6:15)

Our bodies are not just united to Christ in a theoretical sense. Paul says our bodies are members of Christ. The parts of our bodies are now joined to Christ, and we are not at liberty to "unjoin" them when we might want to. For each of us, the parts of our body are now Christ's. We cannot help but take him with us wherever we go and involve him in whatever we do. We have no freedom to reassert ownership of these parts to do with them what we wish or borrow them from him for a time and return them later. Kevin DeYoung writes:

> To put it bluntly, if you shack up with a whore it's like dragging Christ into bed with her too. When you put your faith in Christ, you become one spirit with him (v. 17). So when you put your sexual organs where they don't belong, you are putting the Lord Jesus where he doesn't belong.[3]

We don't get to leave Jesus outside the brothel. If we go in, he goes in with us. For Paul it is simply unthinkable. It should be for every Christian.

We tend to be oblivious to how much we actually matter. Paul's words are a stinging rebuke, but there is unfathomable dignity behind them. The bodies that we so quickly feel ashamed of Christ wants for his own! That truly is amazing. We might want to hide our physical selves from others, but Jesus wants all that we are to be one with him. It's not like he's after our soul but repulsed by our bodies.

Your Body Is a Temple of the Holy Spirit

We come to the other key point Paul's readers need reminding of:

> Or do you not know that your body is a temple of the Holy Spirit within you, whom you have from God? (1 Cor. 6:19)

This is the other side of what we have already seen. We are united to Christ by his Spirit. The Spirit is the means by which he dwells in us and we belong to him.

Again, we can easily become dulled to the immensity of what is being said here. Paul has dropped in that word *temple*, and it is not a low-currency word just to make it all sound a bit more religious. *Temple* to us, if it means anything at all, probably brings up images either of ancient ruins or present-day shrines we may have seen on our travels. If so, for most of us, unless we've come to faith from a background of another major religion, the word *temple* doesn't resonate personally.

The Western Wall of the temple in Jerusalem is part of the surviving structure that had been built by Herod the Great and which would have been there at the time of Christ. It is one of the holiest places to pray for Jews today, who come there to mourn the loss of the temple and all that it represents and to pray for its restoration (hence the wall's older nickname, "The Wailing Wall"). A couple of years ago I had the privilege of visiting it and saw many praying fervently and with evident grief. Such emotional intensity is understandable. An analogy might help.

I remember a car journey as a kid with my parents when we happened to pass a somewhat tatty, nondescript building. We slowed down so my parents could have a good look at it. They were somewhat misty-eyed. The small upstairs apartment had been the first home they'd ever shared. It was obviously inferior to where we were living at the time, but their sentimentality wasn't so much about what it was like as what it *meant*. This was where they had started their life together. Even though they hadn't lived there for many years, and wouldn't have had any desire to, they couldn't help feeling so much affection for the place. It wasn't the quality of the place (evidently!) but the memories. My brother and I no doubt rolled our eyes and waited impatiently to get moving again.

But the reaction would likely be very different if it was a widow or widower driving past. In that case, rather than nostalgia for happy times and memories long displaced by newer and maybe better ones, there'd be the unbearable grief over a life once enjoyed but now tragically unavailable. This, perhaps, takes us a little closer to some of the emotions that were poured out that hot afternoon in Jerusalem. The temple wall we were crowded against wasn't just a place of historic fascination, or even simply a form of shrine. It represented a presence that had in some ways been lost and now mourned, alongside a desperation to have it back again.

A number of thoughts came to me as I watched those fervent pilgrims praying and lamenting. The first was how easily I take my relationship with God for granted. Those men were passionate about God. I am so often indifferent. I can spend whole days being spiritually oblivious.

The second thought that came to me is one I've not been able to shake since my visit there. It keeps coming to me with fresh absurdity. The pilgrims were mourning the loss of their temple.

Standing there among them, I became newly conscious of Paul's words here from 1 Corinthians: "Your body is a temple of the Holy Spirit within you." I'd heard and read these words many times. I knew what they said, inasmuch as I knew the meaning of each of the words. But I hadn't really appreciated the force of their message. Through no merit of my own—only and simply through what Jesus had done—here I was in their midst, *more of a temple than that building could ever or would ever one day be.*

The potential offense of those words hit me. But as I've kept thinking about it, it is nevertheless true. It is not presumption or arrogance. Christ has made it so. *He* has given me *his* Spirit. None of this is on me; all of it is on him. He chooses to make us his dwelling place. It is exactly what he promised:

> I will ask the Father, and he will give you another Helper . . . even the Spirit of truth, whom the world cannot receive, because it neither sees him nor knows him. You know him, for he dwells with you and will be in you. I will not leave you as orphans; I will come to you. . . . In that day you will know that I am in my Father, and you in me, and I in you. . . . If anyone loves me, he will keep my word, and my Father will love him, and we will come to him and make our home with him. (John 14:16–18, 20, 23)

Jesus is promising the gift of the Holy Spirit to all those who come to him. He reassures his disciples that the Spirit will be "another Helper"—that is, another form of what Jesus has already been to them. He is coming, in a way, to take the place of Jesus, to succeed him. He is a really *Jesus-y* Spirit. He is "the Spirit of Christ" (Rom. 8:9).

So the Spirit is not like a substitute teacher, someone who shows up but has a completely different approach, style, set of priorities, and hang-ups. The Spirit is the Spirit of Christ. The departure of Christ would not leave us, as his followers, bereft of all things Jesus. Indeed, this most likely accounts for what Jesus says next: "I will not leave you as orphans; *I will come to you*." The whole point is that we would not be people who are left crying out in inconsolable grief. The gift of the Spirit is the means by which Christ himself comes to be with us, even while he is physically apart from us.

The Spirit is how we enjoy the presence of Jesus. Jesus underlines just how present this Spirit will be in our lives, "the Spirit of truth, whom the world cannot receive, because it neither sees him nor knows him. You know him, for he dwells with you and will be in you" (John 14:17).

The Spirit will be "with you." We will never have to experience a single moment of the Christian life truly alone. Jesus said on another occasion, "I am with you always, to the end of the age" (Matt. 28:20). This is how. It is by his Spirit that he is with us.

This in itself is amazing. But Jesus says more than this. We will not just have the Spirit close by, like a faithful security detail; we will have him *in us*. By this Spirit, God himself comes to dwell in us: "If anyone loves me, he will keep my word, and my Father will love him, and we will come to him and make our home with him" (John 14:23). The Father and the Son dwell in us by the Holy Spirit. Every Christian is the dwelling place of God. But with that comes a new responsibility.

Do you not know that your body is a temple of the Holy Spirit within you, whom you have from God? You are not your own, for you were bought with a price. So glorify God in your body. (1 Cor. 6:19–20)

We began this chapter thinking about these words. In any other context, hearing that we are not our own, that we have been bought with a price, would be devastating. It would indicate a lack of freedom, dignity, and worth. But when applied to Jesus, the opposite is the case. Belonging to him is the only way to true freedom. Nothing could be more dignifying. And nothing shows our worth more than Jesus shedding his own blood for us. To belong to him is the highest and greatest blessing we could ever hope for.

But Paul says it comes with an entailment. Not being our own means our body does not exist solely for our pleasure and agenda. We are to glorify God with it, not ourselves. And this is actually good news. Our body *can* glorify God. For many of us that feels highly counterintuitive. It is a reminder that God is not just interested in the spiritual part of us (which we imagine to be our soul, or spirit), but with all that we are. And so in our body, no less than our mind or heart or anything else, we can bring glory to God. Our body can be a vehicle for the highest purpose in the universe. It can be part of God's own greatest passion project—bringing glory to himself. Our body may be lowly (as Paul says, Phil. 3:21), but it could not have a higher dignity.

9

As a Living Sacrifice

The Body and Discipleship

I RECENTLY MOVED—not just to a new house but to a new country, so everything is new. It has put a new frame around everything I do. It is not that what I do is now all totally different, but the *way* I do everything has changed. I am now doing it all *here*. Even the same things as before now look and feel different.

Coming to Christ changes us. It changes everything. It doesn't mean we do none of the things that we used to do before coming to Christ. We still brush our teeth, take out the trash, and do countless other things. Some things we will no longer do; other things we'll start. But the frame around all of life is now different. My spiritual location has changed. I now belong to Christ. Everything I'm doing, I'm now doing *here*. So what does that look like? What does it mean to honor God with my body? What is it like to be under the ownership of Jesus? Do I need to worry?

No. We already know that Jesus is not a cruel taskmaster. He describes himself in these remarkable words:

Come to me, all who labor and are heavy laden, and I will give you rest. Take my yoke upon you, and learn from me, for I am gentle and lowly in heart, and you will find rest for your souls. For my yoke is easy, and my burden is light. (Matt. 11:28–30)

Jesus recognizes that life in this world, lived according to the ways of this world, is burdensome and wearying. It exhausts us. He has not come to add to that burden or to give us a new but just as unbearable one. He has come to carry our burden, to give us rest, to align our lives the way they were meant to be.

Life in Christ isn't free of obligation. We are to take his yoke upon us and learn from him. But the difference is his heart. He is gentle and lowly. He does not throw his weight around or domineer us. So often the trends within our culture come from a very different kind of heart. The body images commended to us by Hollywood or Madison Avenue fashion houses are presented so that large companies can make a profit. But what Jesus asks from us is always borne from a desire to bless us, not fleece us.

He describes his yoke as "easy." That's not to say that following Jesus is a breeze. It can be difficult. But it means he never treats us in an inhumane way. Paul says of him:

He is the image of the invisible God, the firstborn of all creation. (Col. 1:15)

Jesus is the perfect representation of who God is. He is also the perfect realization of who we're meant to be. We were created to be God's image, and yet we don't do a good job of living it out. We're not very good at being people. But Jesus came to be the perfect human, the full image bearer we have never managed to be. That means he understands true humanity in a way we never will. And it means following him will never be dehumanizing. He will never shrivel up our humanity or diminish us in any way. His ways will always show us how to truly fulfill our humanity.

So we can trust him with our bodies. When we're told to honor God with our bodies, or to offer our bodies to him as a living sacrifice, we needn't be nervous. To commit ourselves to Christ is not to put ourselves at risk of being abused by him. To live for his pleasure is the most healthy and humanizing way we can live with our bodies.

Stewarding Our Bodies

Let's look again at what Paul says to husbands:

> Husbands, love your wives, as Christ loved the church and gave himself up for her, that he might sanctify her, having cleansed her by the washing of water with the word, so that he might present the church to himself in splendor, without spot or wrinkle or any . . . blemish. In the same way husbands should love their wives as their own bodies. He who loves his wife loves himself. For no one ever hated his own flesh, but nourishes and cherishes it, just as Christ does the church, because we are members of his body. (Eph. 5:25–30)

Paul is telling husbands how to love their wives and calling them to model their love on what Christ has shown to his people. The church (as we've seen) is the body of Christ. What is done to the church is, in a way, done to him. When the church is persecuted, Christ can say that he is persecuted (as Paul discovered, Acts 9:4). Paul says this corresponds to the relationship between husband and wife in marriage. The two become one flesh, so failing to love your spouse is like failing to love yourself. Just as you care for yourself, Paul says, you husbands should care for your wives.

At this point Paul makes an assumption about the human body:

No one ever hated his own flesh, but nourishes and cherishes it.

Our first reaction is probably to raise an eyebrow at the first part of Paul's statement. The fact is, plenty of people have hated their own flesh. Someone wrote to me just this week to say that she was considering some radical surgery because she thought it would be the only way she could stop hating her body. Hatred of our own bodies is not uncommon, sadly. In fact, for reasons we've looked at already, all the indications are that bodily hatred is increasing.

It may be best to see Paul's comment as being typically true rather than as always true, without exception. Body-image sensitivities would have been very different in Paul's culture, and I am sure there was significantly less anxiety about such things than there is today. Paul is not denying that people can experience hatred of their own body. He is simply stating that our typical human instinct is to care for our bodies rather than to harm them. This is how we've been designed.

Self-harm is always, therefore, tragic. It is not how we are meant to relate to our bodies. Paul's words are not meant to make us flippant or insensitive when it comes to people self-harming; instead they show us that self-harm is never good. We should never make peace with it, so if it is something we are battling, it is *good* to be battling it.

Self-harm comes in many forms and as a result of many causes. One friend, going through a long season of severe depression and self-loathing, found herself feeling so emotionally numb that she started cutting herself just to feel something. Someone else I know described his self-harm as the physical counterpart to when we might, in frustration at something we've done, say to ourselves, "You idiot!" For this friend, self-harm was a way of expressing that same frustration but in a physical way.

We need to understand the rationality behind self-harm (as best as we can), precisely so we can engage with it and seek to change it. We're meant to look after our bodies rather than doing damage to them.

As Paul makes this aside, he sums up how we should relate to our bodies as nourishing and cherishing them. That is meant to be our default setting. It is worth giving Paul's words some thought, given how unnatural those words might seem for some of us.

Nourishing Our Bodies

Bodies need nourishment. This is not news to us. We're as conscious as we've ever been about the need to provide nourishment in the right way. In fact, we have an overabundance of information about the best ways to feed our bodies. Food packets provide a wealth of nutritional information, much of which, if we're honest, we probably don't understand. We know that too many calories is bad. But then exactly how much potassium or protein we need on a daily basis is beyond most of us.

The Bible seems to be no less attentive to the business of eating, but for very different reasons. There is a surprising amount of teaching in the New Testament on how we eat, what to eat, who we eat with, when not to eat, and times when we shouldn't share a meal with certain other people. For something we might be tempted to think of as merely bodily, there is a lot that is deeply meaningful. We need to learn that "merely bodily" is a contradiction in terms.

Food Is Meant to Be Relational

Food matters in the Bible primarily because eating with others deepens the bonds of friendship. Eating with others has significance. Jesus was criticized not just because he spent time with people known to be sinners, but precisely because he so often ate with them (see, for example, Mark 2:13–16). To eat with known sinners was especially scandalous, because eating suggested identification and acceptance. We tend to be a little more pragmatic and individualistic about meals in our world today. We often eat on the go, or at the office, or on our own at home. So we can easily miss the significance of what is going on with food in the Scriptures. Jesus's "eating with sinners" didn't mean he happened to be seated at the same table with them at Burger King. His dining with them was intentional. In his culture, the food was often eaten communally, with everyone helping themselves from the same dish rather than from individual portions. There was a sense of partnership and communality that we tend not to think about, at least in Western culture. For us, food is about fueling for the next several hours. Then, it was much more about relationship.

This is why there are times when it is not appropriate to eat with someone:

> But now I am writing to you not to associate with anyone who bears the name of brother if he is guilty of sexual immorality or greed, or is an idolater, reviler, drunkard, or swindler—not even to eat with such a one. (1 Cor. 5:11)

Jesus ate with sinners because he came for sinners and wanted to invite them to follow him in repentance and faith. Paul is talking about those who claim to be doing that but who are refusing to turn away from sin. He is not so much talking about Christians struggling with sin (which is all of us), but those claiming to be Christian who *persist* in sin. There is discussion as to whether this prohibition is limited to church meals or whether it also applied to the Christians individually. There are arguments for both sides.[1] The point for us is how this illustrates the fact that eating with people says something about your standing with them. Food is not just biological, but relational.

Food Is Meant to Be Pleasurable

Food is also meant to be about enjoyment. So Paul warns against those who

> forbid marriage and require abstinence from foods that God created to be received with thanksgiving by those who believe and know the truth. For everything created by God is good, and nothing is to be rejected if it is received with thanksgiving. (1 Tim. 4:3–4)

Food is part of the creational good that is given by God as a gift to us. Paul says it is to be "received with thanksgiving." It is an expression of not just God's provision but also of his kindness. Food is flavorful, not just nutritious, because it is meant to be *enjoyed* and not just absorbed.

That is not to say there are no dangers in the other direction. If rejecting the goodness of food is one problem, so too is greed. Anything good can become an idol, if we put it front and center where it doesn't belong, and we can easily turn food into an idol when we make its pleasure a source of the kind of comfort and redemption that only God can bring. Kevin DeYoung (following C. S. Lewis's lead) notes that the problem of gluttony is "not too much food, but too much attention to food."[2] So being overly fussy is as much a problem as being overly indulgent. It is easy to think not eating certain things is the key to fullness of life. Pleasure and self-control are not mutually exclusive.

To give careful thought to what and how we eat is not unspiritual. Our bodies need to be nourished. Food is given for this, and for it to happen in a way that is both enjoyable and relational.

Cherishing Our Bodies

When talking to husbands about loving their wives just as they would love their own bodies, Paul also says that our bodies should be cherished. Feeding them is a significant part of how we care for our bodies, but it is not the only part. We need to look after our physical health. This comes up elsewhere in Scripture:

> While bodily training is of some value, godliness is of value in every way, as it holds promise for the present life and also for the life to come. (1 Tim. 4:8)

Paul's main focus here is obviously on the importance of godliness. But the fact that godliness has greater value doesn't change the fact that bodily training still has *some* value. Paul is not advocating the former *instead* of the latter, but in *addition to it*. Godliness is of supreme value, but that is not to say physical exercise is of *no* value. Sure, if we make physical exercise ultimate, we have turned it into an idol and are not actually stewarding our bodies for the Lord in the right way. But prizing godliness shouldn't mean we are indifferent to our physical health. A healthy lifestyle is an appropriate way to care for the bodies God has given us.

There can be a tendency to neglect these things.

Sleep

It is easy to overlook sleep and think it unspiritual. But the Bible speaks of it, and commends the importance of resting well. Sleep is a gift from God:

> It is in vain that you rise up early
> > and go late to rest,
> eating the bread of anxious toil;
> > for he gives to his beloved sleep. (Ps. 127:2)

Trying to squeeze as much productivity out of the day—early starts and late nights—does not ultimately make us more productive. We need sleep. Pushing ourselves beyond what is healthy will only (according to the psalm) be "in vain." We won't end up accomplishing more. It is "anxious toil," which is not trusting in God but in our own efforts. Neglecting rest is often a sign that we are not truly trusting God enough to stop working. As Victor Hugo wrote, "Go to sleep in peace. God is awake."[3] Or as King David said:

> In peace I will both lie down and sleep;
> > for you alone, O Lord, make me dwell in safety. (Ps. 4:8)

The Bible also warns us against too much sleep. If too little sleep can be a sign that we are not trusting God, too much can be a sign of being lazy:

> I passed by the field of a sluggard,
> > by the vineyard of a man lacking sense,
> and behold, it was all overgrown with thorns;
> > the ground was covered with nettles,

and its stone wall was broken down.
Then I saw and considered it;
    I looked and received instruction.
A little sleep, a little slumber,
    a little folding of the hands to rest,
and poverty will come upon you like a robber,
    and want like an armed man. (Prov. 24:30–34)

The property of the sluggard is in disrepair because he is sleeping when he should be up and working. His land (a field or vineyard in the proverb) is his means of income; neglecting it will lead quicker than he realizes to poverty.

But it is not just a matter of being productive in our work. Being well rested is also essential to our spiritual health. Too little sleep dulls our senses and awareness. We are less spiritually alert to resist temptation, less attentive to what God is saying in his word. Our minds wander more than normal when we pray. We find it harder to concentrate at church. Sleep is a spiritually significant matter. If it is something God "gives to his beloved," then we need to receive it with thanksgiving and steward that gift wisely.

Robert Murray M'Cheyne was a significant preacher in Scotland in the early nineteenth century, but his fruitfulness was bound up with overwork and exhaustion, and he died shortly before his thirtieth birthday. As he was dying, he reportedly said, "The Lord gave me a horse to ride and a message to deliver. Alas, I have killed the horse and cannot deliver the message." Had he better stewarded his body, he might have had many more years in which to preach the message of Christ.

Stewardship of our body matters. It belongs to Christ. It is not unspiritual to think about our health, diet, rest, and exercise.

Disciplining Our Bodies

In his letter to the Corinthians, Paul has been explaining how all he does is driven by the gospel. He has been culturally flexible where needed, identifying with both Jews and Gentiles as appropriate. He has waived what would have been a perfectly appropriate right to be paid for his Christian ministry. Paul is willing to give up his rights for one reason: he wants the message of the gospel to go forward:

> We have not made use of this right, but we endure anything rather than put an obstacle in the way of the gospel of Christ. (1 Cor. 9:12)

Paul's willingness is admirable. But he is also at pains to point out that it was not automatic. Paul's gospel determination did not come about without significant commitment on his part:

> Do you not know that in a race all the runners run, but only one receives the prize? So run that you may obtain it. Every athlete exercises self-control in all things. They do it to receive a perishable wreath, but we an imperishable. So I do not run aimlessly; I do not box as one beating the air. But I discipline my body and keep it under control, lest after preaching to others I myself should be disqualified. (1 Cor. 9:24–27)

Paul appeals to something he expects his readers to know. For most people today, the biggest sporting event on the calendar is the Olympic Games. There is no other event that involves more athletes from more countries. For Paul's readers, one of the sporting highlights would have been the Isthmian games, held there in Corinth every two years, attracting huge numbers of visitors and attention.

Paul draws attention to two particular elements: running and boxing. In the case of running, Paul points out that there is only one victor: everyone competes, but only one wins. And so the only way to win is by being determined. This involves more than just running every once in a while. Athletes, Paul says, have to be self-controlled "in all things." The rest of life has to be organized around the priority of competing. In his day, there was physical training, dietary constraints, and lifestyle choices, all of which shaped the capacity of the runners to compete effectively. There was intentionality and determination—all so that they could win a "perishable wreath," a crown made by weaving withered celery.[4] They didn't even get a gold medal. But the prize was a sufficient honor and of sufficient worth that they were willing to make whatever sacrifices were needed in order to obtain it.

That same kind of intentionality and determination is to mark Christians too. There is a key difference: our prize is eternal and not perishable. The wreath worn by the victorious Corinthian would deteriorate at some point. It would not last. But the prize for the Christian is everlasting. Paul does not spell out exactly what that prize is, but there are some significant clues as to what he is talking about. He has just summarized his ministry in these words:

> I have become all things to all people, that by all means I might save some. I do it all for the sake of the gospel, that I may share with them in its blessings. (1 Cor. 9:22–23)

Elsewhere he talks about the prize this way:

> Not that I have already obtained this or am already perfect, but I press on to make it my own, because Christ Jesus has made

me his own. . . . I press on toward the goal for the prize of the upward call of God in Christ Jesus. (Phil. 3:12, 14)

Paul's striving is not about trying to gain Christ by his own efforts, but about having Christ and wanting the fullness of all that is in him. This speaks to the other key difference: when it comes to athletic competitions there is only one winner, but the prize Paul speaks of here is not only eternal, but within the grasp of all believers who are willing to focus their energies on obtaining it. Each of us, with sufficient self-control, can receive our reward from Christ.

This is where the body comes in. Winning this prize means not "running aimlessly." We are not going to win accidentally—as though we could find ourselves at the end of a leisurely jog being awarded an Olympic gold medal. It will happen only with commitment. And the opposite of running aimlessly is spelled out:

But I discipline my body and keep it under control, lest after preaching to others I myself should be disqualified. (1 Cor. 9:27)

Successful athletes discipline their bodies. They live by strict regimens. Everything is weighed according to whether it will help or hinder them in their pursuit of victory. The same is true for Paul. He will not obtain the prize without going into rigorous battle with his own body. Paul is not saying that the body is intrinsically bad and needs to be punished. But he is saying many of its impulses need to be resisted if we are to move forward toward triumph. It will not happen without this kind of discipline. Paul knew so much of this from his own experience. His commitment to sharing the gospel had significant physical costs:

Five times I received at the hands of the Jews the forty lashes less one. Three times I was beaten with rods. Once I was stoned. Three times I was shipwrecked; a night and a day I was adrift at sea. (2 Cor. 11:24–25)

The temptation to hold back, as he considered a new ministry opportunity, must have been considerable. He knew there would be hostility. He knew there could be yet more intense physical pain. A huge part of him must have been thinking, "I've done enough. I can't cope with more of this." The body was certainly pulling against him. So Paul had to fight those physical impulses to back off from full commitment to the gospel.

The same is true for us, in a variety of ways. Most of us do not face that kind of physical pain. But we do have bodily wants and desires that need to be constantly resisted if we are to move forward with Christ. If we go with our physical instincts, without questioning and resisting them, we will drift away from the prize. Paul's final words here are a sober warning:

I discipline my body and keep it under control, lest after preaching to others I myself should be disqualified. (1 Cor. 9:27)

Paul is keeping with the athletics analogy. In major games like the Olympics there are those who end up disqualified. They fail a drug test or collude in some form of match fixing. They have to go, and they leave the contest in disgrace. And just as the prize for the Christian is so much more valuable than for the athlete, so too the prospect of disqualification is all the more awful. Paul is about to warn his readers, "Let anyone who thinks that he stands take heed lest he fall" (1 Cor. 10:12). We all need this warning. The

Bible—and subsequent church history—is littered with cautionary tales of those who seemed spiritually vibrant but in the end showed themselves to be disqualified.

The key to it all is the body. It needs to be disciplined. It needs to be kept under control. If we only ever go with the wants, desires, and appetites of our bodies, we will not continue in Christ. Body control is part of the self-control all of us are called to. So how are we to do this? We have already seen that the body is "for the Lord, and the Lord for the body" (1 Cor. 6:13). The best way to use our bodies rightly is to use them for Christ. They are to be given wholly over to his service.

Offering Our Bodies

Paul has spent eleven chapters of his letter to the Christians in Rome explaining the jaw-dropping grace of God seen in all that Jesus has done for us. At the start of chapter 12 he starts unpacking how we should respond. Christian living is in response to what God has done for us (rather than an attempt to earn it). It also shows us the work of Jesus will have a radical impact on our lives. He comes to us as we are, showing us lavish and undeserved love. But he won't leave us as we are—we are now his people, living in the sunny uplands of his kindness to us. So Paul summarizes all that comes next in the Christian life:

> I appeal to you therefore, brothers, by the mercies of God, to present your bodies as a living sacrifice, holy and acceptable to God, which is your spiritual worship. (Rom. 12:1)

Paul instructs us to present our bodies to God, to offer them to him. Paul makes very clear that this is in response to what God has done. We don't offer God our bodies *so that* he might love us; we offer our bodies because he has *already* loved us first in Christ. This is how we are to respond to all God's mercies.

In other words, the offering we make is about more than bodies. When Paul says "present your bodies," he is talking about all of life. As he goes on in the next few chapters to unpack what this means, it is clear he's talking about something far more encompassing than just physical behavior. That the word *body* can summarize and denote all of life shows us just how central the body is to Paul's understanding of who we are. But while the word *body* isn't restricted to our physical bodies, it obviously includes them. John Stott writes, "No worship is pleasing to God which is purely inward, abstract and mystical; it must express itself in concrete acts of service performed by our bodies."[5] So as believers, we are to present our bodies to God. This is only fitting given that Paul has already told us our bodies belong to God.

Offering ourselves to the Lord is "spiritual worship," according to Paul. The word *spiritual* carries the sense of being reasonable. Offering ourselves is not an arbitrary way to respond to God's grace; it is the only rational and sane thing we can do in light of all that he has done for us. Anything less would make no sense. Given what God has done, we eagerly surrender our whole selves to him, pledging all that we are to his service.

Just as we are not to offer our bodies in some clinical way that is all duty and no devotion, so also God does not receive them with indifference. Paul says that our giving ourselves to God is "holy and acceptable" to him. That is, it is pleasing to God. This is so significant. I don't know what physical imperfections most trouble you about your body, but surely there is something because none of us is a perfect physical specimen. These imperfections are, for some, just a given in life and not necessarily something to be unduly troubled by. But for many, physical flaws can eat away at us and become a life-dominating struggle.

One of the biggest British movies in the 1990s was the comedy *The Full Monty*, about a group of unemployed men in the north of England who decide to become male strippers. One of them, Dave, is overweight, and in a moment of doubt says to his wife, "Look at me. Who wants to see *this*?" It is a sentiment many of us might echo. We feel self-conscious about our body precisely because we suspect it would not be pleasing to others if seen. But a body offered to God is a body that is pleasing to God. You do not have to be a physical Adonis. Virtually no one is. But you can have a body pleasing to the Lord if it is consecrated to him in grateful service. He will never reject us or the body we offer to him.

So what does it look like to offer our body to God? Paul has already spelled it out:

> Let not sin therefore reign in your mortal body, to make you obey its passions. Do not present your members to sin as instruments for unrighteousness, but present yourselves to God as those who have been brought from death to life, and your members to God as instruments for righteousness. (Rom. 6:12–13)

Paul puts it in the negative and then in the positive. Sin is not to reign in our body. It once did, before we belonged to Christ. But now *Christ* reigns in us. With this transfer of ownership comes the transfer of each part of our body. The "members" are not to be presented to sin to be used for an unrighteous agenda. No, they are to be presented to God for *his* agenda.

Paul shows us why and how this switch of allegiance can be made: "Present yourselves to God as those who have been brought from death to life." We have been made new. We continue (for now) in the same body we have always had. It doesn't look immediately different when we become Christians. But we have changed. God has given us new birth by the Spirit. We have a new self (Eph. 4:24). It is as though we are running new-creation software on old-creation hardware. And so we take the parts of our body and offer them to God.

We still wait for the redemption of our body. It will be made new too, in due course (as we will see in the next chapter). But that does not mean it is a spiritual write-off until then. Even now—today—the parts of our body can be "instruments for righteousness."

It is worth thinking through literally. How can the various parts of our body be offered to God? John Stott puts it like this:

> Our feet will walk in his paths, our lips will speak the truth and spread the gospel, our tongues will bring healing, our hands will lift up those who have fallen, and perform many mundane tasks as well like cooking and cleaning, typing and mending; our arms will embrace the lonely and unloved, our ears will listen to the cries of the distressed, and our eyes will look humbly and patiently towards God.[6]

When we really consider it, the possibilities are almost endless. It does us good to imagine the ways our body can be used in the service of God.

This is true even for those experiencing significant physical constraint. Perhaps we are unable to get around as easily as others, or we might even be housebound. We may be tempted to think we're not much use to God. But it is worth remembering that Paul spent a significant portion of his life in a comparable situation—imprisoned by the Romans. We don't always know the full details of what that would have involved, whether it was house arrest or being in a prison cell, but Paul spoke often of his chains, and he certainly wasn't free to move around as he would have wanted. And yet he was able to serve God profoundly under such circumstances. He wrote a number of our New Testament letters from jail. We know he prayed faithfully and thoroughly for the Christians he knew (or only knew of) in various places around the world. And we know he shared the gospel with those around him, with prison guards coming to know of Jesus (see Phil. 1:13). Paul was physically restrained, but in his mind's eye he roved around the world, thinking of different churches and their needs and considering how he might encourage and pray for them. And he knew that the gospel message itself was not in chains; it was journeying its way around the Roman Empire through Paul, even while he himself was immobilized (see 2 Tim. 2:8–9). *Any body* can be offered to God for his service, whether we're fighting fit or bound to our bed.

None of this should surprise us, of course. Paul had already shown the Roman Christians that their sinfulness had been evidenced in the ways they used the parts of their bodies. He'd summarized the plight of humanity in this way:

> None is righteous, no, not one;
>> no one understands;
>> no one seeks for God.
> All have turned aside; together they have become worthless;
>> no one does good,
>> not even one. (Rom. 3:10–12)

This is all of humanity, apart from Christ. It is a somber assessment. But Paul goes on to give evidence: he describes how various parts of the body are characterized:

> "Their throat is an open grave;
>   they use their tongues to deceive."
> "The venom of asps is under their lips."
>   "Their mouth is full of curses and bitterness."
> "Their feet are swift to shed blood;
>   in their paths are ruin and misery,
> and the way of peace they have not known."
>   "There is no fear of God before their eyes." (Rom. 3:13–18)

Throats, tongues, lips, mouths, feet, eyes—all reflecting the reality that we do not (left to our own devices) know or understand God. This is what it looks like for sin to "reign in your mortal body" and to present "members to sin as instruments for unrighteousness" (Rom. 6:12–13). So it is wondrously fitting for our new allegiance to Christ to show in how we now use those same parts of the body, offering them to God to be used for his purposes.

We need to know this. In too many areas of our discipleship we have separated our Christianity from our bodies. There are aspects of our physical life that we think are irrelevant to our faith, and there are parts of our Christian life that we think have nothing to do with our bodies.

The truth is that the New Testament often speaks of discipleship in bodily terms, and in ways that tend to surprise us. Aspects of life we might not even think about, such as eating and dressing, the New Testament has much to say about (as we have already seen). These things are not trivial or spiritually irrelevant. The problem many of us have is that we are oblivious to their spiritual significance; we don't see them as part of our discipleship and service to God.

Similarly, there are areas of our Christian life where we tend to think the body is not involved. I speak very much as a white man from England, a demographic not known for bodily expressiveness. When it comes to something like prayer, for example, it is easy to think it is simply a matter of our inner self. The body is not involved, other than perhaps to close our eyes so that we can focus on praying. So it is striking how often the Bible speaks of bodily posture when describing prayer. It does so in a variety of ways.

We read of people lifting up their hands in prayer (Ps. 28:2); raising their eyes in expectation (Ps. 121:1), or lowering them in contrition (Luke 18:13). We also see David sitting to pray (2 Sam. 7:18), Paul kneeling to pray (Eph. 3:14), and John prostrating himself with his face to the ground (Rev. 1:17). No one posture is prescribed. But it goes to show that prayer is not a matter of bodily indifference. Our posture can help express or encourage the appropriate posture of our heart.

The same goes for corporate worship. Again, much of my experience has been shaped by a culturally conservative English lack of expressiveness. We're meant to sing with enthusiasm and joy, but the unwritten rule is that while our hearts, minds, and mouths are engaged, our bodies aren't, other than the fact that we stand to sing. I am guilty of having thought like this. I'd experienced a lifeless and very traditional church during my time at university that was big on physical choreography but small on Christ himself. We would stand, or bow, or face east for certain parts of the liturgy. The pastor would make a big deal of kissing the Bible before the Gospel reading, even though he was quite open about not fully believing in its message. It left me with a revulsion for anything that looked like religious theatrics. But I overreacted. The problem was not that they used the body in worship, but that they used it hypocritically, failing to express what should actually have been a heart attitude. In overreacting the way I did, I threw the baby out with the bathwater.

There is a reason that even in that same culturally conservative, inexpressive England, men still go down on one knee to propose. Asking for someone's hand in marriage is about as formal a moment as we can experience. It really matters. It is a sign of deference, of humility, of the worthiness of the person being asked and the lack of presumption of the one asking. If a man asked with his hands in his pockets, something would be seriously off. The posture is meant to match the heart. It is as much of a mismatch when the posture of our body doesn't match the posture of our heart as when (like at the church I attended at university) the posture of our heart doesn't match the posture of our body. If we wouldn't keep our hands in our pockets at a football game, it seems incongruous to do so at church.

What we do with our bodies matters. And what we don't do with our bodies also matters. People from a similar background to mine do well to reflect on the fact that corporate worship in the Bible is far more physically expressive than the worship in our own churches tends to be. Even allowing for the natural variety God has given us in temperament, it suggests that the determined non-use of our bodies in worship isn't neutral but unbiblical.

10

To Be Like His Glorious Body

The Body and the Resurrection to Come

THE MASAI MARA. The Grand Canyon. The Great Barrier Reef. These are, according to a TV show a few years ago, three things you must see before you die. Actually, they're just three out of fifty. Not only was the BBC show *50 Places to See Before You Die* popular, but books with titles like that have been on best-seller lists ever since.

In fact, the show seems to have spawned an entire new genre. As well as things to see before death, there's a host of other things to add to the list: "100 Things to Do Before You Die," which includes getting a tattoo and milking a cow; "100 Things to Eat Before You Die," such as a hot dog (fairly easy to get hold of) and crocodile (perhaps harder). The idea has become a growth industry. Dozens of books and websites urge you to complete their lists, offering albums to listen to, movies to watch, sensations to experience. And the lists go on.

That this genre has all been so successful reveals something significant about us. It highlights what has become a great concern for many. We want to experience the best of what's out there before it's too late. It's a first-world problem: for those of us who don't worry about putting a roof over our heads or food on the table, our greatest fear seems to be getting to the end of life and feeling we've not gotten our money's worth.

According to an article in the *New York Times*, one of the main culprits is "Instagram Envy."[1] The nature of a site primarily for sharing pictures is that it tends to be the really nice pictures people share—that particularly attractive meal, holiday scene, or cute moment with the kids. The cumulative effect of all these images is that our own normal lives look pretty drab by comparison. We're left with the impression that everyone else's life is more glamorous and pleasurable than our own.

And it's all feeding into the ever-growing pathology, fear of missing out (FOMO to those who know about such things)—an anxiety prevalent enough to be the subject of study by a group of Oxford psychologists. We're increasingly desperate not to miss the best of what's out there and plagued by the fear that we might. Life is short. The world is big. We only get one shot. The perspective of the Bible is very different. Yes, the world is big. And, yes, this life is short. But this life is not all there is.

It is both curious and revealing that we human beings seem to find life uncomfortably short. The sense of not having enough time, of our typical life span being inadequate, of even death in old age coming too soon—it's all unique to us. We live far longer than some creatures (fruit flies tend to stick around for just a couple of weeks), and far shorter than others (some sharks and whales can live for a couple of centuries). But we seem to be the only creature with an unshakable sense of the shortness of life. Something inside of us feels there is meant to be more.

In the midst of his extraordinary suffering, Job saw something of this feeling. As he sat in agonizing pain, with no prospect of relief before death, something in nature nagged away at him:

> For there is hope for a tree,
>> if it be cut down, that it will sprout again,
>> and that its shoots will not cease.
> Though its root grow old in the earth,
>> and its stump die in the soil,
> yet at the scent of water it will bud
>> and put out branches like a young plant. (Job 14:7–9)

Nature is full of such examples. I visited some friends and went to look at one of their garden plants that I enjoy seeing, only to discover they had cut it down to the very ground. A few stumps barely poking out of the soil were all that was left. Yet when I came back a couple of weeks later, the plant had burst back to life and full flower, very much open for business for the bees that were diligently attending it.

Job uses the example of a tree, which too can be reduced to a stump. And yet its apparent death is not the end. New shoots can appear, and in time many more buds and branches. There is hope for trees. But not, so it would appear, for people:

> As waters fail from a lake
>> and a river wastes away and dries up,
> so a man lies down and rises not again;
>> till the heavens are no more he will not awake
>> or be roused out of his sleep. (Job 14:11–12)

It is a perplexing observation. It is hard for Job to accept that with so many apparent examples in nature of life beyond seeming death, humans would simply die and be no more. The natural world around us is full of rumors of resurrection. Job is left with a sense that surely there must be more to come. What Job hoped for with only limited understanding the New Testament outlines in far more detail.

I'm not a fan of camping. To be fair, I've only done it properly once, in Scotland, which is hardly noted as a climate conducive to sleeping outside. I'm immediately skeptical of the quality of any accommodation that I can carry on my back. In any case, the whole point of vacation for me is not to find a manner of living that is *less* comfortable than normal life would be back home. Going from a home with hot showers, air-conditioning, and a bed to something lacking all of these is a downgrade, not an improvement. The apostle Paul seems to agree:

> We know that if the tent that is our earthly home is destroyed, we have a building from God, a house not made with hands, eternal in the heavens. For in this tent we groan, longing to put on our heavenly dwelling, if indeed by putting it on we may not be found naked. For while we are still in this tent, we groan, being burdened—not that we would be unclothed, but that we would be further clothed, so that what is mortal may be swallowed up by life. (2 Cor. 5:1–4)

Paul was no stranger to tents—he made them. So he knows what they can do and what their limitations are. He uses them here as an illustration for our physical lives in the present age. And notice what he says about these bodily "tents" in which we all live: they can be destroyed—they're vulnerable. Paul knew that. His body had already been wrecked by the rigors of ministry and the opposition he had encountered. He also talks about these tents being temporary. They're not eternal. Nothing we do with them can change that. The most any of us might do is lengthen our lives. But while we might delay death, we can never avoid it. Our bodies die.

But our inevitable death stands in contrast to the life to come that God has promised us. Whereas life now is lived in these vulnerable and temporary tents, God has promised us a "building," "a house not made with hands, eternal in the heavens." We will go from a tent to a building. From a life of groaning and being burdened to fullness. From less clothed to more clothed. All this language points in one unmistakable direction: the life to come is going to be more real than our lives here.

We often labor under the misunderstanding that the life to come will be some vague form of nonphysical existence. If we have any image of it, it is of something almost ghostly, floating around as spirits. But the vision the Bible has for us is not wraithlike but physical. And the evidence and template for this physical life to come is the resurrection of Jesus. The Bible is clear about what happened to the body of Jesus following his death:

> I delivered to you as of first importance what I also received: that Christ died for our sins in accordance with the Scriptures, that he was buried, that he was raised on the third day in accordance with the Scriptures, and that he appeared. (1 Cor. 15:3–5)

Jesus physically died. He was physically buried. And he physically rose again. He went on to experience new bodily life after his death. None of that is left field. His resurrection, just as his death, was according to Scripture. This is how it was always going to be. It is not uncommon to hear people interpret Jesus's resurrection as some kind of "spiritual" happening, by which Jesus was still, in some nonphysical way, present with his disciples following his death. But this is not what the accounts present to us. Jesus was *physically* raised. His physical resurrection points to our own:

> But in fact Christ has been raised from the dead, the firstfruits of those who have fallen asleep. (1 Cor. 15:20)

Jesus's resurrection is not an isolated event. It is the starting gun for the resurrection of all who follow him. The firstfruits are the initial batch of a crop to materialize. Their significance for the farmer is that they are the sign and guarantee that the rest of the harvest is not far behind. That *this* portion of the harvest has appeared is a sign that much more is to come.

So it is with the resurrection of Jesus. His resurrection is the first of many, which means that we have a physical, bodily life promised to us in the age to come. Paul puts it this way:

> If the Spirit of him who raised Jesus from the dead dwells in you, he who raised Christ Jesus from the dead will also give life to your mortal bodies through his Spirit who dwells in you. (Rom. 8:11)

The resurrection of Jesus makes our own resurrection as his people a certainty.

This promise of a physical resurrection life after death often surprises Christians. Many of us have an image in our minds of simply "going to heaven" when we die. So what actually does happen to us?

The Bible doesn't necessarily answer every question we might have about death or provide every detail, but it does provide clear teaching on what happens when we die. Paul's reflections on his own life and possible immanent death show us his own expectations of what would happen:

I am hard pressed between the two. My desire is to depart and be with Christ, for that is far better. But to remain in the flesh is more necessary on your account. (Phil. 1:23–24)

Paul expects to be taken into the presence of Jesus when he dies. This fits with Jesus's own promise to the thief on the cross who was executed with him: "Truly, I say to you, today you will be with me in paradise" (Luke 23:43). When believers die, they go to be with Christ in heaven. Paul describes this prospect as being "far better" even than continued and fruitful life on earth. Christ is with us now, as he promised to be throughout our earthly discipleship (Matt. 28:20), but at death we will be in his presence in a far more glorious way.

For all this splendor, being with Christ in heaven is not our final destination. Disembodied existence in heaven is not God's ultimate plan for us; it is physical, resurrection life in the new creation we await. Those who have already died in Christ are not yet in their final condition. Going to heaven is a temporary glory before the final and greater glory of the new heavens and the new earth is realized.

What Will Our Resurrection Bodies Be Like?

Paul anticipates this question when he writes:

But someone will ask, "How are the dead raised? With what kind of body do they come?" (1 Cor. 15:35)

Perhaps we can't help but wonder. Once we start imagining what it will be like, the questions come flowing. What age will we all be in these resurrection bodies? Will we be the ages we were when we died or all the same age as each other? Will my body still have some of the features about it I don't like, or will it be *exactly* what I've always wished?

It is natural to wonder. But it is foolish to worry (as Paul makes clear in the first part of his answer in 15:36, below!). It can lead to skepticism. And it is foolish to disbelieve something simply because our limited imaginations can't fully picture it. Paul gives us good evidence for believing in the resurrection body to come:

> You foolish person! What you sow does not come to life unless it dies. (1 Cor. 15:36)

Nature is full of examples of life from apparent death. Every time we plant a seed, we're burying it in the ground. It goes through a symbolic death. And yet it comes to life. A plant grows. And growth can *only* happen because the plant first dies. Leaving the seed in its packaging leads to nothing. It has to die first. So to think the idea of a human body going into the ground and one day rising to new life is not as ridiculous as it might seem. As with the seed, our bodies have to die so that they can be raised.

Paul doesn't stop there. There's more than that business of planting seeds shows us:

> What you sow is not the body that is to be, but a bare kernel, perhaps of wheat or of some other grain. (1 Cor. 15:37)

Think about it. Most seeds do not remotely resemble the plant they will eventually grow into. If you show me a mix of various seeds for different vegetables, I doubt very much I would be able to tell just from their appearance which vegetable each seed will eventually produce. It doesn't work like that. Part of the agricultural process is the complete transformation of the seed into what it will become. Before and after look completely different. What emerges from the ground is out of all proportion to what was put into it.

Paul then takes a wide-angle look at the natural world:

> Not all flesh is the same, but there is one kind for humans, another for animals, another for birds, another for fish. There are heavenly bodies and earthly bodies, but the glory of the heavenly is of one kind, and the glory of the earthly is of another. There is one glory of the sun, and another glory of the moon, and another glory of the stars; for star differs from star in glory. (1 Cor. 15:39–41)

When you look around at the multiplicity of life in the natural world and up at all that goes on in the heavenly world, it is obvious that there is a staggering range of physical bodies God has made. He is not limited in his scope or capacity. There are some musical artists whose work always sounds exactly the same, however many songs they release. They clearly have a limited creative range. But this is not so with God. His physical creativity is boundless. Each creature has the body it needs, and each heavenly body has its own unique glory. So we should not think that it is beyond this God to create resurrection bodies for us to enjoy in the age to come.

So far, Paul has given us good reason not to be skeptical about our resurrection bodies. But what will they actually be like? The best way to know something of what our bodies will look like is to look at the risen Christ. We will be raised with the kind of body he has been raised with. Just as our bodies now corresponded to

Adam's—becoming a vehicle for sin—so our new bodies will correspond to the resurrection body of Jesus:

> Just as we have borne the image of the man of dust, we shall also bear the image of the man of heaven. (1 Cor. 15:49)

> [He] will transform our lowly body to be like his glorious body. (Phil. 3:21)

We can expect something of the same continuity and difference between our present and future bodies that was evident with Jesus's resurrection body. When he was raised, he was still recognizably Jesus. He still bore the scars of his crucifixion and broke bread with his disciples much in the way he had done before. But he was also different, seemingly able to pass through closed doors and appear and disappear at will.[2] So we will be like ourselves now—recognizably us—while also possessing capabilities we presently lack. Paul spells out some of these new differences for us:

> So is it with the resurrection of the dead. What is sown is perishable; what is raised is imperishable. It is sown in dishonor; it is raised in glory. It is sown in weakness; it is raised in power. It is sown a natural body; it is raised a spiritual body. If there is a natural body, there is also a spiritual body. (1 Cor. 15:42–44)

Paul contrasts our present bodies with how they will be raised. That our bodies now are perishable is so painfully obvious to us. Attempts at trying to maintain an ever-youthful appearance are always rather pathetic. The reality always catches up with us. We age and decay, but the body to come will be eternal. It will not gradually wear down. Our bodies now are marked by dishonor. As we've seen, they're marked by sin—our own and that of others. We cannot escape that. But the body to come will have an untarnished glory. Our bodies now are weak. I am in my mid-forties and already feeling some of the limitation that comes with age, compared to twenty years ago. But the new body will have undiminishing power. My body now is "natural"—it is of the nature of this present world. But the body to come will be "spiritual," not meaning nonphysical, but gloriously fitted to the new creation that God is preparing. It will be the perfect vehicle to glorify God.

It is this that makes the future body so wonderful. We might be tempted to think that a resurrection body will be great because it will finally mean a flat stomach or a full head of hair, or any number of other imperfections made right. But the real glory is not that our future bodies might conform to our present culture's view of beauty in some particular way (at least better than our present bodies do), but that with these new bodies we will be able to glorify and serve Jesus perfectly. That is what should make us most excited.

Knowing all this can give us a new way to look at our lives. The fact is, this body now, in all the ways in which it is a blessing and a burden, is not the only bodily experience we will ever have. Through Christ we are confident of a future resurrection. There will be no more physical temptations, no more spiritual or physical weakness. No more shame or affliction. No more sin. And no more death. In terms of this life I am beginning to be past my prime. But my best physical days actually lie ahead of me rather than behind me. I don't need to constantly look back on past glories or bemoan the encroaching limitations of age.

This is the answer to our deep fear of missing out. I don't need to worry about squeezing every last drop of pleasure out of this physical life when I can look forward to an eternity of enjoying the new creation in a resurrected body. If I never get to see those things we're all meant to see before we die—that's fine. There is no urgency. Other things matter much more, and I'm not ultimately going to miss out on anything. I'd love to see the Grand Canyon in the US, or the Southern Alps in New Zealand, but I don't *need* to. There is no need to live for the pleasures of this world.

You may be someone who experiences chronic pain. I find such an experience hard to imagine. There may be no hope of relief in this life. But this life is not all there is. I know a man who has near-constant severe migraines. There is little to no relief, no treatment that seems to have much effect. But he can be assured, through faith in Christ, that there will be a physical life to come without that relentless pain. Or I think of the wonderful Christian Joni Eareckson Tada, paralyzed from the neck down and confined to a chair since a diving accident when she was seventeen. Now over seventy, she has said that the first thing she plans to do with her new resurrection body is to fall on her knees before Christ in worship.

One of my hobbies, when walking through old settlements in England with time to kill, is to take a look at some of the gravestones in the local churchyard. I was strolling through one just a few days ago, visiting the new tombstone for my grandmother's grave. Her headstone looked conspicuously clean. Many of those around were crumbling and leaning, their plots overgrown with grass and weeds. As I looked around, many of the inscriptions had long since worn down to the point of illegibility. But many were still possible to read.

One word that appears on gravestones of a certain age is the Latin word *Resurgam*. (It turns up on someone's grave in *Jane Eyre*.) This translates as "I shall rise again." It is a message of defiant confidence.

The grave may be our destination, but it is not our destiny. There is risen life to come. In airline terms, it is like a transit lounge, a place where we wait between legs of our journey, but not our final destination. Wherever that may be for each of us, and for however long we may end up there, each of us can say, "I shall rise again!"

Death is no longer a threat in the way it was. It has been defeated in Christ. The signs of aging are no longer a threat but a promise. Gray hair and deepening lines on my face don't need to speak to me of a past I can't recover but of a future I can barely conceive. The real glory days are not behind but ahead.

The poet George Herbert said, "Death used to be an executioner, but the Gospel makes him just a gardener."[3] You don't bury a Christian; you plant him. One day to arise in perfected physical glory. Perhaps the final words should go to C. S. Lewis:

> These small and perishable bodies we now have were given to us as ponies are given to schoolboys. We must learn to manage: not that we may some day be free of horses altogether but that some day we may ride bare-back, confident and rejoicing, those greater mounts, those winged, shining and world-shaking horses which perhaps even now expect us with impatience, pawing and snorting in the King's stables.[4]

Acknowledgments

THIS PROJECT BEGAN about three years ago, at the home of the Roe family in Shincliffe, County Durham, UK. The bulk of it was completed in the very same home during the Covid-19 lockdown in the late spring and summer of 2020. I am, as always, both grateful for and dumbfounded by your kindness. Thank you. Your home is a wonderful place to write and think and to be distracted from writing and thinking by my captivating godson, Ned.

I have had the opportunity of teaching some of this material on a number of occasions. Particular thanks to St. Mary's Church, Maidenhead; The Village Church, Denton; and the Cru Winter Conference in Baltimore. The interactions and honesty after each talk helped enormously.

I am grateful to the team at Crossway for shepherding this book and its tardy author through the publishing process, and to Lydia Brownback especially for her sterling work as an editor. Austin Wilson continues to be invaluable as a literary agent.

Friends helped me along the way by reading sections of the book and providing invaluable feedback. Thanks especially to Rebecca McLaughlin, Harrison Elkins, Lou Philips, and Ryan Sprague for your insights, suggestions, and encouragement.

Finally, to the elders and church family at Immanuel Nashville, to whom this book is dedicated. Thank you for being such a faithful embodiment of a gospel community. It is an honor to serve among you. At the climax of one of my favorite movies, *When Harry Met Sally*, Harry comes to his senses and interrupts Sally in the middle of an event and blurts out, "When you meet someone you want to spend the rest of your life with, you want the rest of your life to start as soon as possible."[1] It is how I feel about you. Thank you for upholding a culture of honesty, safety, joy, hospitality, and honoring one another. Special thanks to pastors Ray Ortlund and T. J. Tims for the countless ways you encourage me. Time with you both in Ray's study has been a highlight of the past year. I love you, brothers.

Notes

Chapter 1: Fearfully and Wonderfully Made

1. C. S. Lewis, *Mere Christianity* (1952; repr. New York: HarperCollins, 2001), 98.
2. C. S. Lewis, *That Hideous Strength* (1945; repr., New York: Scribner, 2003), 170.
3. Ernest Cline, *Ready Player One* (New York: Crown, 2011), 57.
4. Thomas Page McBee, "Until I Was a Man, I Had No Idea How Good Men Had It at Work" accessed November 5, 2020, https://getpocket.com/explore/item /until-i-was-a-man-i-had-no-idea-how-good-men-had-it-at-work?utm_source= pocket-newt.
5. I am grateful to my friend Bethany Jenkins for drawing my attention to this.
6. Zack Eswine, *Sensing Jesus: Life and Ministry as a Human Being* (Wheaton, IL: Crossway, 2012), 186.
7. Eswine, *Sensing Jesus*, 183.
8. Eswine, *Sensing Jesus*, 186.

Chapter 2: Man Looks on the Outward Appearance

1. Andrew Wilson, "Ink and Identity," *Think* website, June 17, 2015, http://think theology.co.uk/blog/article/ink_and_identity.
2. H. Wheeler Robinson, in Paula Gooder, *Body: Biblical Spirituality for the Whole Person* (London: SPCK, 2016), 34.
3. Carl Trueman, "The Triumph of the Social Scientific Method," *First Things*, June 15, 2020, https://www.firstthings.com/web-exclusives/2020/06/the-triumph-of -the-social-scientific-method.
4. Gooder, *Body*, 41.
5. See Gooder, *Body*, 32–41.
6. Sherif Girgis, Ryan T. Anderson, and Robert P. George, *What Is Marriage?: Man and Woman: A Defense* (New York: Encounter, 2012), 24; emphasis original.
7. "If a man ruins your car, he vandalizes your property, but if he slices your leg, he injures *you*." Girgis et al., *What Is Marriage?*, 24.
8. Girgis et al., *What Is Marriage?*, 24.
9. Alastair Roberts, "The Music and Meaning of Male and Female," *Primer* 03, Gender and Sexuality (Market Harborough, UK: Fellowship of Independent Evangelical Churches, 2016), 41.

10. An observation made by Matthew Lee Anderson, *Earthen Vessels: Why Our Bodies Matter to Our Faith* (Bloomington, MI: Bethany House), 92.

11. Peter J. Leithart, *The Baptized Body* (Moscow, ID: Canon Press, 2007), 5.

12. N. T. Wright, *Creation, Power and Truth: The Gospel in a World of Cultural Confusion* (London: SPCK, 2013), 9.

13. Wright, *Creation, Power and Truth*.

14. Trueman, "The Triumph of the Social Scientific Method."

15. Michael Jensen, *You: An Introduction* (Sydney, AU: Matthias Media, 2008), 51.

Chapter 3: Male and Female He Created Them

1. Rob Smith, "Responding to the Transgender Revolution," *The Gospel Coalition* website, accessed July 3, 2020, https://www.thegospelcoalition.org/article/responding-to-the-transgender-revolution/; emphasis original.

2. Pairings are not incidental to the account of creation in Genesis 1. It is full of them—heaven and earth, light and darkness, sun and moon—and this male-female pairing represents the climax of the creation story.

3. I am grateful to Andrew Wilson for this observation.

4. Smith, "Responding to the Transgender Revolution."

5. Alastair Roberts, "The Music and Meaning of Male and Female," *Primer* 03, Gender and Sexuality (Market Harborough, UK: Fellowship of Independent Evangelical Churches, 2016), 29.

6. Ray Ortlund Jr., *Marriage and the Mystery of the Gospel* (Wheaton, IL: Crossway, 2016), 17.

7. Roberts, "The Music and Meaning of Male and Female," 30.

8. Ray Ortlund Jr., "Male-Female Equality and Male Headship," in *Recovering Biblical Manhood and Womanhood: A Response to Evangelical Feminism*, ed. John Piper and Wayne Grudem (Wheaton, IL: Crossway, 2012), 97.

9. Ortlund, *Marriage and the Mystery of the Gospel*, 18.

10. Tim Keller, "The Bible and Same Sex Relationships: A Review Article," accessed December 22, 2016, http://www.redeemer.com/redeemer-report/article/the_bible_and_same_sex_relationships_a_review_article.

Chapter 4: God Formed the Man

1. It is worth pointing out that the word "helper" here is not meant to mean anything demeaning—it is also used in the Bible to describe how God is *our* helper.

2. I am grateful to Jen Wilkin for the observations in this paragraph.

3. C. S. Lewis, "Priestesses in the Church?," in C. S. Lewis, *God in the Dock* (Grand Rapids, MI: Eerdmans, 1970), 260.

4. C. S. Lewis, *Perelandra* (1943; repr., London: HarperCollins, 2005), 253.

5. Timothy Keller with Kathy Keller, *The Meaning of Marriage: Facing the Complexities of Marriage with the Wisdom of God* (New York: Dutton, 2011), 200.

6. Jen Wilkin, "General Session 2," Advance 2017 conference, hosted by Acts29 US Southeast, accessed June 28, 2020, https://vimeo.com/243476316.

7. Angus MacLeay, *Teaching 1 Timothy: From Text to Message* (Ross-Shire, UK: Christian Focus, 2012), 99.
8. Sam Andreades, *Engendered: God's Gift of Gender Difference in Relationship* (Wooster, OH: Weaver, 2015), 132; emphasis original.
9. See the observation by Eric Metaxas in *Seven Women and the Secret of Their Greatness* (Nashville: Thomas Nelson, 2015), *xviii–xix*.
10. G. K. Chesterton, "Comparisons," *Poetry Nook* website, accessed December 1, 2020, https://www.poetrynook.com/poem/comparisons-4.

Chapter 5: Subjected to Futility
1. J. R. R. Tolkien, *The Lord of the Rings* (London: Allen & Unwin, 1954).
2. Michael J. Fox, *Lucky Man: A Memoir* (London: Ebury Press, 2002), 4.
3. Matthew Lee Anderson, *Earthen Vessels: Why Our Bodies Matter to Our Faith* (Bloomington, MI: Bethany House, 2011), 88.

Chapter 6: The Body Is Dead Because of Sin
1. The New International Version of the Bible tends to translate such references to "the flesh" as "the sinful nature" for this reason. See Douglas Moo's personal explanation in Douglas J. Moo, *Encountering the Book of Romans: A Theological Survey* (Grand Rapids, MI: Baker Academic, 2002), 127.
2. Gordon D. Fee, *The First Epistle to the Corinthians*, New International Commentary on the New Testament (Grand Rapids, MI: Eerdmans, 1987), 259–60.
3. Roy E. Ciampa and Brian S. Rosner, *The First Letter to the Corinthians*, Pillar New Testament Commentary (Grand Rapids, MI: Eerdmans, 2010), 264.
4. Matthew McCullough, *Remember Death: The Surprising Path to Living Hope* (Wheaton, IL: Crossway, 2018), 19.
5. McCullough, *Remember Death*, 35.
6. *The Beach*, screenplay by John Hodge, based on the novel by Alex Garland, Figment Films, 2000.
7. *The Beach*.
8. McCullough, *Remember Death*, 36.
9. C. S. Lewis, *That Hideous Strength* (1945; repr., New York: Scribner, 2003), 241.
10. Bill Bryson, *The Body: A Guide for Occupants* (London: Doubleday, 2019), 9.
11. Timothy Keller, *On Death (How to Find God)* (New York: Penguin, 2020), 3.
12. Bryson, *The Body*, 12.

Chapter 7: A Body You Have Prepared for Me
1. Dane C. Ortlund, *Gentle and Lowly: The Heart of Christ for Sinners and Sufferers* (Wheaton, IL: Crossway, 2020), 47.
2. Ortlund, *Gentle and Lowly*, 49.
3. Timothy Keller and Kathy Keller, *The Meaning of Marriage: A Couple's Devotional* (New York: Viking, 2019), 282.
4. Keller and Keller, *Meaning of Marriage*, 282.
5. Ortlund, *Gentle and Lowly*, 212.

Chapter 8: A Temple of the Holy Spirit

1. Roy E. Ciampa and Brian S. Rosner, *The First Letter to the Corinthians*, Pillar New Testament Commentary (Grand Rapids, MI: Eerdmans, 2010), 428.

2. Ciampa and Rosner, *First Letter to the Corinthians*, 254.

3. Kevin DeYoung, *The Hole in Our Holiness: Filling the Gap between Gospel Passion and the Pursuit of Godliness* (Wheaton, IL: Crossway, 2012), 112.

Chapter 9: As a Living Sacrifice

1. See, for example, the commentary in Roy E. Ciampa and Brian S. Rosner, *The First Letter to the Corinthians*, Pillar New Testament Commentary (Leicester, UK: Apollos, 2010), 218.

2. Kevin DeYoung, "But What about Gluttony!?!," *The Gospel Coalition* website, April 24, 2014, https://www.thegospelcoalition.org/blogs/kevin-deyoung/but-what-about-gluttony/.

3. I am grateful to Ray Ortlund Jr. for highlighting this to me.

4. Ciampa and Rosner, *First Letter to the Corinthians* (Leicester, UK: Apollos, 2010), 439–40.

5. John Stott, *The Message of Romans* (Nottingham, UK: InterVarsity Press, 1994), 322.

6. Stott, *Message of Romans*, 322.

Chapter 10: To Be Like His Glorious Body

1. Alex Williams, "The Agony of Instagram" *New York Times*, December 15, 2013, https://www.nytimes.com/2013/12/15/fashion/instagram.html.

2. John 20:26; 21:1; and Luke 24:31.

3. Cited in Timothy Keller, *On Death* (How to Find God) (New York: Penguin, 2020), 72.

4. C. S. Lewis, *Miracles: A Preliminary Study* (1947; repr., New York: HarperCollins, 2001), 266.

Acknowledgments

1. *When Harry Met Sally*, directed and produced by Rob Reiner, Castle Rock Entertainment, July 14, 1989.

General Index

Adam: creation of, 41–42; naming the animals, 71–72
Adam and Eve: ate the forbidden fruit, 111–12; creation of, 70, 71; shame of, 97–98
aging, as promise not threat, 185
already and not yet, 12
Anderson, Martin Lee, 95
Andreades, Sam, 83
artisanal products, 25
asceticism, 141
athletes, 162–65
Avatar (film), 49–50

Beach, The (film), 113–14
beauty, 127, 129–30; culture's view of, 183; fantastical expectation of, 95
belonging to Christ, 138, 150, 151
Bible: given to men and women, 71–72; on the soul, 42–44
biological sex, 58; and gender, 59
biology, as meaningful, 57
bodies of death, 109
bodily brokenness, 60, 64, 88–94, 99, 102, 118, 120, 131–34; of Jesus, 99, 124–25, 131–32, 138
bodily healing, 94, 127
bodily sin, 103–10
bodily training, 158

body/bodies: as accidental, 27; cherishing, 158–60; and curse of the fall, 131; discipline of, 161–65; exchange of, 23; as fallen, 60; fearfully and wonderfully made, 24–25, 28, 29, 60, 104; frailties of aging, 25; as a gift, 21–23, 37; and glorifying God, 150; gratitude for, 28–29; and identity, 51–52; inseparable from who we are, 44; as "instruments for righteousness," 168; as interchangeable, 50; intrinsic to identity, 41, 42, 45; as intrinsically good, 104; "knitted together," 25; limitations of, 22, 25, 33; as living sacrifices, 153, 165–66; for the Lord, 142; as malleable, 40; as members of Christ, 107, 144–45; as mere property, 45; not everything, 46–49; not nothing, 49–51, 172; not in opposition to the soul, 44; nourishing of, 155–58; personally made, 25, 27; purposefully made, 26–27; relevance to God's purposes, 141; seeing through the lens of the gospel, 12–13; and spiritual matters, 15; stewardship of,

Scripture Index

Also Available from Sam Allberry

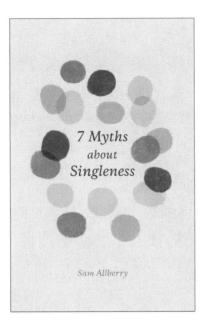

"The local congregation must be not merely a
loose network of families but a close-knit family
itself, consisting of both married couples and
singles, all living together as brothers and sisters.
This volume will show us how to do that."

TIMOTHY KELLER, Founding Pastor, Redeemer Presbyterian Church,
New York City; Chairman and Cofounder, Redeemer City to City

For more information, visit **crossway.org**.